D1559614

Texas

MYTHS & LEGENDS

LEGENDS OF THE WEST SERIES

TEXAS

MYTHS & LEGENDS

THE TRUE STORIES BEHIND HISTORY'S MYSTERIES

SECOND EDITION

DONNA INGHAM

LONE
STAR
BOOKS

Guilford, Connecticut

LONE STAR BOOKS

An imprint and registered trademark of Rowman & Littlefield

Distributed by NATIONAL BOOK NETWORK

Copyright © 2016 by Rowman & Littlefield
Map: Alena Pearce © Rowman & Littlefield

All rights reserved. No part of this book may be reproduced in any form or by any electronic or mechanical means, including information storage and retrieval systems, without written permission from the publisher, except by a reviewer who may quote passages in a review.

British Library Cataloguing-in-Publication Information Available

Library of Congress Cataloging-in-Publication Data Available

ISBN 978-1-4930-2612-8 (paperback)
ISBN 978-1-4930-2613-5 (e-book)

∞™ The paper used in this publication meets the minimum requirements of American National Standard for Information Sciences—Permanence of Paper for Printed Library Materials, ANSI/NISO Z39.48-1992.

To Stephanie, the best choice our son ever made

CONTENTS

ACKNOWLEDGMENTS

First I must acknowledge the folklorists who have, over many years, collected and passed on tales of buried treasure, larger-than-life and unexplained creatures, ghostly visitations, mysterious phenomena, and legendary people. Many of these tales are preserved in the *Publications of the Texas Folklore Society* and provided the starting place for much of my research. From there I was aided by librarians, members of historical societies, chamber of commerce directors, archivists, and countless other individuals who were eager to tell what parts of a story they knew. And, of course, if Globe Pequot hadn't invited me to take on the project in the first place, I likely would never have gone chasing after these fourteen mysteries and legends and worked with editors Meredith Rufino, Greg Hyman, Linda McLatchie, and Courtney Oppel. Any book of this sort is a collaborative effort. I would be remiss if I did not also credit my husband, Jerry, first reader and willing field research partner, and my son, Christopher, always a patient and knowledgeable giver of technical and moral support.

INTRODUCTION

No matter how sophisticated we think we are, we're still drawn to the mysteries and legends around us—accounts of things that are as yet unexplained or unsolved. Every region has its own, but the tales seem to fall into familiar categories: lost treasures, legendary creatures or places that have fantastic attributes, haunted sites, and mysterious people. Rounding up over a dozen mysteries and legends of Texas, exploring their roots and sources, and speculating about the "truth" of them has been a challenging and enlightening project.

With no premeditation on my part, the chapters in this book seemed to come together in twos and threes: rumors of treasures like those buried by Jean Lafitte along the Texas Gulf coast and those discovered and then lost in silver mines in the Texas Hill Country; legends about the exploits of a white ghost buffalo and a pacing white stallion on the Texas plains; reported sightings of cryptid creatures identified as bigfoot and chupacabra in south and east Texas; accounts of mysterious sights and sounds at natural wonders such as Enchanted Rock and Mitchell Flat near Marfa; ghost stories still circulating in "haunted" cities like Jefferson and San Antonio; and mysteries associated with people such as Sally

Skull, possibly a murder victim; Chipita Rodriguez, an accused ax murderer hanged in San Patricio; and Frenchy McCormick, a widow who stayed by her man and became the last living inhabitant in a Panhandle ghost town.

As suggested in the listing above, I did make a conscious attempt to provide some geographical diversity in the gathering of stories. So there are tales from the Gulf coast, from parts of south Texas, from the southwestern Big Bend country, from the plains of west Texas, from central Texas, from east Texas, and from the Texas Panhandle. Some tales involve greed and later hopes for redemption; some inspire apprehension or simply curiosity; some represent symbols of freedom and independence; some include violence and murder; and one is an outright love story.

Each chapter in this collection begins with a legend or a reported mysterious occurrence and then offers background and what explanations are currently available in primary source documents, secondary research material, and firsthand interviews. Bibliographies of print and online sources are included.

At least one interesting set of connections emerged during the research process. Jim Bowie, who figures in the chapter on the lost San Saba Mine, knew and did business with the privateer Jean Lafitte, the central figure in another chapter. According to one story, Bowie brought treasure with him to the Alamo in San Antonio, as mentioned in yet another chapter. Most of the legends and mysteries detailed in the book have been part of Texas folklore since the nineteenth century or before, but reports of chupacabra sightings are fairly recent and continue to be breaking news stories as people try to decide whether the creatures are a new species or merely rural versions of urban legends. Researchers, meanwhile, continue to pursue serious studies into the possibility that Texas bigfoot creatures do exist. The speculation goes on. And so do the folktales. These are just a representative sample. Enjoy.

CHAPTER 1

Jean Lafitte's Treasures

In February the Texas Gulf coast is cold and blustery. The air has a damp chill that penetrates clear to the bone. On just such a day back in the 1880s, an old Confederate war veteran, cold and weary, rode through the fading twilight near La Porte looking for shelter.

Just as the moon was rising, he saw the silhouette of a house and, before that, a stable. The old soldier led his horse into the stable, unsaddled him, and tied him there; then, carrying his saddle and blanket, the traveler approached the house.

"Hello!" he called. "Is anyone there?" The only answers came from the howling wind and the crashing surf. He tried the doors. Locked. He found a window that he managed to open, and he crawled inside the house.

"Hello!" he called again. No answer.

By the light of a struck match, he could see that he was in a large room with a fireplace. Beside the fireplace was a stack of wood, and before long he had a fire going. He stood close to absorb the heat and then spread his saddle blanket on the floor. The saddle itself would be his pillow and his rain slicker his cover. Tired as he was, he had hardly lain down before he was asleep.

He couldn't say how long he'd slept when he suddenly awoke, knowing that someone else was in the room with him, looking at him. By the dim light of the fire, he saw the figure of a man standing, staring, and somehow beckoning. The man, handsomely fitted out in tailored britches and a short jacket with wide lapels, stood still as death, his eyes unblinkingly arrogant. Yet those eyes had an appeal that caused the old soldier to get up and follow his eerie visitor out of the warm room, through the next room, and into a third. This room was small and barren. The cracks in its walls allowed the wind to whistle and moan its way inside.

The ghostly figure spoke: "It is here," he said, stopping in the middle of the room. "It is here that more gold lies buried than is good for any man."

Shivering now, the old veteran looked at the bare floor.

"You have but to dig," the specter continued, "and it is yours. I cannot use it. You can. However, it must be applied only to good purposes. Not one penny may be spent for evil or selfish reasons. You must keep the faith; you must not fail on this point. Do you accept these terms?"

"Yes," the veteran answered, and his visitor was gone. Still the specter's words, "more gold . . . than is good for any man," hung in the air, and the weary traveler made his way back to put more wood on the fire and think his situation over. Before long, he dozed off again.

And again he awoke to find the ghostly visitor staring down at him. Not so much in anger as in reproach, the specter said, "I need your help more than you can know, and yet you fail me."

"The treasure is mine to give," he continued. "I paid for it with the substance of my soul. I want you to have it. With it you can right the balance and remove somewhat the burden of the guilt I carry because of it. You can give me peace."

Once more the specter beckoned, and once more the veteran followed him to the spot where the treasure was buried. This time the veteran would swear he could see revealed to him great quantities of gold and jewels, a treasure beyond anything he had ever dreamed of as a boy. For growing up he had heard the tales about Jean Lafitte's buried treasures and had planned one day to search for them. With growing certainty, he now believed that his visitor was, in fact, the ghost of the pirate Lafitte.

The ghost spoke once more: "Do not force me to come again." Then he was gone.

The traveler thought about the treasure and the restless spirit who could find no peace. But mostly he thought about the words, "more gold . . . than is good for any man." He returned to the fire.

Not really rested, but now more anxious than tired, he put on his slicker and gathered up his saddle and blanket. He went out to saddle his horse, aware that the wind was still wailing and the waves were still crashing. Across the chilly bay, however, he could just make out the slightest promise of light. The prospect of dawn had never been more welcome.

The old veteran mounted up and rode away—away from the ghost of Jean Lafitte and away from the treasure, away from "more gold . . . than is good for any man."

With or without the addition of guardian ghosts, could any of the many tales about Jean Lafitte's buried or sunken treasures be true? Those tales single out practically every inlet, cove, and island along the 367 miles of the Texas Gulf coastline as a possible resting place for chests full of jewels and Spanish doubloons or stacks of gold and silver bullion. And this fabled treasure still draws people to come with their tools to dig in the shifting sands on Galveston Island and Padre Island, along the rest of the Gulf coast, and at the mouths of rivers flowing into the Gulf of Mexico.

Stories like the one about the haunted house in La Porte have been passed down orally and collected by folklorists for years in Texas, continuing to fuel the treasure-hunting fever. The prelude to the La Porte story, as recounted by Julia Beazley in *Publications of the Texas Folklore Society* (1924), says that Lafitte and his crew anchored their schooner in Galveston Bay opposite the house in question and that Lafitte and two of his men rowed ashore with a heavy chest aboard their skiff. As soon as the skiff grounded on the beach, watchers from the anchored schooner saw Lafitte blindfold his two helpers before the three disappeared. Two hours later Lafitte returned alone and in a black mood. Too frightened to ask where their comrades were, the remaining men aboard the schooner assumed Lafitte had killed them to make sure no one would know the exact whereabouts of the treasure. Shortly thereafter, according to the legend, the buccaneers left the Galveston Bay area for good, and the cache has never been discovered or retrieved.

Beazley claims in her account of the tale that it was told to her "by a Confederate veteran who has now passed on." Ann Malone, former president of the La Porte Bay Area Historical Society, confirms that the Beazleys were early settlers in La Porte and had a house on Galveston Bay, about where Sylvan Park is today. That house was struck by lightning a long time ago and burned to the ground, she said. As to the other house, the haunted one, Malone said that such a house probably existed at one time, but it's not there anymore. A clerk in the bait shop on Sylvan Beach said that he still occasionally sees people wandering around the park with metal detectors but that in recent years the area hasn't seen any real treasure-hunting frenzy.

Still, La Porte lays claim to "our pirate" and published a version of the haunted-house legend in an article in its Diamond Jubilee Publication in 1964. The article also notes that "one man from a far distance came to seek the cache but after a single night on the spot, quickly abandoned his plans." From time to time, the article says, a few gold coins have been found in the waters off Morgan's Point, just to the north, and in the Bay Ridge area, where Lafitte supposedly anchored his schooner. La Porte, a city of just over 30,000 people, is about thirty-five miles north of the city of Galveston, where Lafitte established his Texas headquarters.

Although much about the life of Jean Lafitte remains uncertain or contradictory, it is fairly well documented that he set himself up as the master of Galveston in 1817, succeeding another privateer named Louis Michel Aury. (Lafitte much preferred the term *privateer* over *pirate*, because *privateer* carries with it some slight degree of legitimacy.) In essence, privateers were sanctioned looters of enemy ships, and Lafitte had the blessing of the ruling Mexican government to go after all the Spanish ships he could catch in the Gulf. The problem was that his men weren't always careful to check which flag was flying on captured ships.

Lafitte, accompanied by his brother Pierre, came to Galveston with experience in lawlessness, having first been a smuggler and freebooter in Louisiana. Pursued and threatened by authorities there, he gained a pardon by offering his services to the United States in the War of 1812 with England, and he aided Andrew Jackson in the battle of New Orleans, on January 8, 1815. Having agreed not to reestablish his base of operations in Louisiana, Lafitte scouted for another location and moved to Galveston Island.

On the island he set up a conclave he called Campeche, or Campeachy, and built Maison Rouge (Red House), a two-story building facing the inland harbor. It too is the subject of a legend. According to the story, Lafitte struck a deal with the Devil, promising that if the Devil would build the house, Lafitte would deliver to the Devil the first thing he laid eyes on the next morning. Then Lafitte had one of his men throw a dog in his tent at first light, and that dog was all the Devil got for his trouble.

By early May 1820 Lafitte was once again being hounded by authorities bent on shutting down his Texas establishment, so he abandoned Campeche within a year and burned his compound to the ground. The remnants of the Maison Rouge foundation are still visible, along with the ruins of another building constructed over it in 1870, at 1417 Avenue A (Water Street), near the wharf in Galveston. Lafitte sailed on his flagship to Isla Mujeres, just northeast of the Yucatán Peninsula, and continued his illegal activities until his death around 1825 or 1826.

The details of both his birth and death are disputed and have become part of the mystery of his life story. Some biographers claim that he was born in Bayonne or Bordeaux, France, probably

JEAN LAFITTE.

Jean Lafitte may have left buried treasure along the Texas Gulf coast.
COURTESY OF THE ROSENBERG LIBRARY, GALVESTON, TEXAS

in 1780 or 1781. Others say that he was born as early as 1776 or as late as 1790, and they name a variety of other locations—such as Saint-Malo, Pauillac, or Brest in France; Orduna in Spain; or Saint-Domingue (now Haiti)—as possible birthplaces. One biographer even argues for Westchester, New York. By way of documentation, the 1813 registration for Pierre Lafitte's ship *Goelette la Dilidente* names Jean Lafitte as captain and lists his age as thirty-two and his birthplace as Bordeaux, France.

Although most biographers agree that Lafitte died on Yucatán or on an island off its coast, the circumstances of his death are uncertain. Most speculate that he died of an illness, but others describe a more romantic and adventuresome departure from this life: One legend has him rescuing Napoleon from exile, burying the French national treasure somewhere near Port Isabel or Brownsville, and both of them dying in Louisiana; other stories suggest that Lafitte's own men killed him shortly after they left Galveston or that his entire force perished off Yucatán in a hurricane in 1826; still another tale claims that he changed his name and simply disappeared.

More than one writer has drawn a parallel between Lafitte and the protagonist in Lord Byron's "The Corsair," published in 1814. The closing couplet of that narrative poem does seem fitting for a man recognized among many as a gentleman and onetime war hero who plied the pirate's trade: "He left a Corsair's name to other times, / Linked with one virtue and a thousand crimes."

Perhaps Lafitte's most lasting legacy is the abundance of stories describing the buried or sunken treasures he left behind. According to legend, much of the booty is still there for those lucky enough or clever enough to discover it. Yet no one has ever reported finding any.

Most of the loot was supposed to have been buried on Galveston Island. L. D. Lafferty, a contemporary of Lafitte's, recalled that Lafitte "frankly confessed that he had enough silver and gold on the island to freight a ship." Lafitte also reportedly said that he had left enough gold buried in Texas to build "a solid gold bridge across the Mississippi River."

Author Gary Cartwright admits to having searched for the legendary Three Trees on Galveston Island, a landmark mentioned as long ago as the sixteenth century by Cabeza de Vaca in his diary. The trees were later a gathering place for the Karankawas, who, Cartwright says, in 1817 "fought a bloody three-day battle with Jean Lafitte's pirates." Rumors persist that Lafitte buried some gold at the Three Trees site, and, with the help of a Galveston constable, Cartwright finally found what is now marked as Lafitte's Grove on private property in West Beach, between Galveston and Freeport. "Over the years," Cartwright says, "Islanders have turned up small caches of treasure, a few doubloons here, a few coppers there, nothing to speak of." Yet he couldn't resist the temptation to dig the toe of his boot into the soft dirt, just in case.

Two other groves of trees, near where the Lavaca River enters Galveston Bay, are said to be markers for finding buried treasure. Legend says that Lafitte took a compass reading and a bearing on the two groves, called the Kentucky Motte and the Mauldin Motte, after he and two of his men had buried a chest filled with gold coins and jewelry and two canvas sacks filled with silver bars. He made notes in his journal and drove a long brass rod into the ground above the treasure. He never returned.

Years later, so the story goes, a hired hand watching over some horses and cattle on the grassy marshes near the groves found the tip of the brass rod, pulled it out of the ground, and took it to the ranch headquarters. The rancher, a man named Hill, was familiar with the tale of Lafitte's buried treasure. The two men returned to search the area, but they couldn't find the spot where the rod had been. Then in 1870 a turkey hunter found what he thought was a pile of bricks. He picked up one brick and took it with him, only to discover later that it was a bar of pure silver. He too was unable to find the cache when he returned.

One man, however, may have found Lafitte's buried treasure chest. Called Crazy Ben, he was an eccentric street character in the 1880s in Galveston and claimed to be an old pirate. He wore an earring and paid for drinks at the waterfront bars with gold doubloons. He had no apparent means of income and lived in a shack near the mouth of the Lavaca River. His story was that he had once been Jean Lafitte's cabin boy and had witnessed the burying of the treasure marked by the two groves of trees. After he was certain that Lafitte was not coming back to retrieve the gold, Crazy Ben began to make withdrawals from the chest.

In time, some of those who heard the story followed Crazy Ben in hopes of finding the gold themselves. Apparently, Ben eluded them, until one night when two shadowy figures tracked the staggering Ben as he headed back to his shack. The next morning his body washed up on the shore. Crazy Ben's throat had been slashed, and no one knows what happened to the treasure.

Another potential treasure island along the Texas Gulf coast is Padre Island, southwest of Galveston. The northerly dune range of that island is said to contain a fortune marked by a legendary "millstone," and at least one writer thought he had found it. Ed Syers, author, historian, and newspaper columnist, kept a driving log of a trip he and a friend, Gene French, made on Padre Island in the 1970s. Setting out from Corpus Christi in Betsy, French's "cabover, four-wheel-drive pickup," the two men intended only to do some beachcombing and some surf fishing.

When they reached mile 39.5, however, Syers made this notation:

Rested Betsy. By accident, uncovered at dune edge, lip of 150-lb., 3-foot diameter, perfect circle concrete slab, 6 inches thick. Treasure hunters take note. Meets specifications for Lafitte's legendary Padre millstone. We dug like terriers, even skeptical French, found nothing. Lafitte's treasure, believed a five figure fortune, was cached under a millstone . . . how many sand-shifting hurricanes back?

Sunken treasures, some still in their ships or on wagons, are said to be in Matagorda Bay, in the gumbo mud of Hendricks Lake, in the brackish Sabine Lake, or in the Gulf itself. Some of those treasures are said to be guarded by ghosts, though less welcoming than the one in La Porte.

Still, perhaps less frequently now, groups of treasure seekers come, some financed with big money and equipped with sophisticated equipment. They search from low-flying aircraft and even try dowsing. They are serious and optimistic, believing that somewhere—if not beneath the shifting sands and the salt grass of Gulf beaches and river marshes, then perhaps below a highway, a building, or a public park—they will unearth buried riches.

It should be noted here that Texas has very strict laws protecting all artifacts, treasure, and other objects buried beneath its domain. And those who go exploring on Padre Island National

Seashore must go without their metal detectors because the National Park Service prohibits the possession or use of such devices in the park "in order to preserve cultural resources." In fact, if anyone comes upon any kind of cultural artifact on the island, he or she is supposed to note the location of the object and notify a park ranger. That would, no doubt, include chests full of gold and silver and jewels.

CHAPTER 2

The Lost San Saba Mine

The year was 1756. Don Bernardo de Miranda, lieutenant-general of the province of Texas, was leading a Spanish military expedition northwest from the village of San Fernando (present-day San Antonio). They were looking for minerals, especially precious ones like gold and silver, and they were trying to determine how many Indians were in the area. It was slow going back in those days, especially in February in the rain, and they had traveled only about ninety miles in eight days when they set up camp near Honey Creek, which fed into the Llano River.

Most of the men were happy to rest themselves and their horses in camp, but Miranda and some of the would-be miners in the expedition decided to go exploring. They crossed the Llano River and began scouting north. After traveling some fifteen or twenty miles, they came to a low red-colored hill on the San Saba River and began investigating the canyons and ravines extending from it. They came across a natural cavern in one of them. Miranda took a few of his soldiers and stepped inside. They hadn't gone far with their lighted torches when they saw it: silver, in thick veins. The riches were here, just as they had hoped.

The minute Miranda got back to San Fernando, he filed a report with his superiors in Mexico City describing the silver discovery in the cave he named La Cueva de San Jose del Alcazar and including samples of the ore. In his report Miranda predicted that the mines in the Cerro del Almagre (Red Hematite Hill) "are so numerous that I guarantee to give to every settler of the province of Texas a full claim. . . . The principal vein is more than two varas in width and in its westward lead appears to be of immeasurable thickness." A *vara* is a measure of length varying between about thirty-two inches to about forty-three inches, so the vein of silver would have been wider than six feet. As evidence of his findings, he produced more than three pounds of ore to be assayed. It tested at about ten ounces per hundredweight. Miranda pressed for permission to set up a *presidio*, a fortress for protection from Indian attack, and to begin mining and smelting the silver. Before the permission came, however, he was sent on another military expedition to the missions near the Sabine River in east Texas and never returned to command the presidio or to realize any riches from the mine he claimed to have discovered.

The wheels of government continued to turn, however slowly, and a presidio was finally established, actually to protect a mission, not far from the San Saba River, but quite a distance from Miranda's silver-laden cavern. First called San Luis de las Amarillas and later Real (Royal) Presidio de San Saba, the fortress was apparently undermanned and undersupplied; as it turned out, it didn't even effectively protect the Mission Santa Cruz de San Saba. The mission priests, meanwhile, claimed that the Lipan Apache they hoped to convert to Christianity had been working a silver mine of their own in the nearby hills. Before long, legend has it, the priests too got into the mining and smelting business, until a warring party of Comanche, some 2,000 strong, attacked the mission in 1758 and killed all but two people. That marked the end of the Spanish-Mexican government's search for silver in the area, and the mine or mines were lost.

Or were they? For that matter, did they ever exist in the first place?

Easily the best known searcher for the lost San Saba mines was Jim Bowie, destined to be remembered for his distinctive knife and as one of the fallen heroes at the Alamo. According to one story, Bowie heard about silver brought by Lipan Apache to San Antonio. He was determined to find its source. Reportedly, Bowie befriended the Apache chief Xolic, gifting him with an expensive rifle. He lived among the Apache until he was regarded as a brother. In time Bowie learned the whereabouts of the Apache silver mine and abandoned the tribe to return to San Antonio. There he mounted his own expedition in 1831 to mine the silver. Camped at the site of the old Spanish mission, by now in ruins, Bowie and his men supposedly extracted large quantities of ore from the Apache's mine and hauled it by burro to San Antonio. However, Bowie's treasure seeking was thwarted by attacking Apaches, whom Bowie had allegedly betrayed. Somewhere along Calf Creek or Silver Creek, Bowie and his party had to take cover and fend off the attack, which lasted for several days. They lost one man, and the rest made it back to San Antonio. Whatever long-term mining plans Bowie might have had ended on March 6, 1836, when he died at the Alamo.

Jim Bowie's name is often linked to the lost San Saba mine.
THE STATE PRESERVATION BOARD, AUSTIN, TEXAS

Also in the early 1830s a man named Harp Perry and several Mexicans brought twelve burro loads of silver bullion into San Antonio, converted the silver to coins, and made large deposits in area banks. Reportedly, Perry and a couple of his friends operated a mine near the Little Llano River, extracting mostly silver but also finding some gold in nearby rocks. They built a crude smelter some distance from the mine and poured molten silver and gold into molds made from hollowed-out cane growing along the river bottoms. Perry and his partners are said to have buried some of the bullion—up to 1,200 pounds of it—in the area. They marked the site by pounding a big rock into the knothole of a large pin oak tree near the cache and in a direct line from a spring.

The Comanche, once again unhappy to see their traditional hunting grounds overrun with settlers and determined to drive the newcomers out, put a stop to Perry's operation. In 1834 a large war party attacked the miners. Only Perry and two others escaped. Perry went south to Mexico, married, and lived comfortably on his deposited wealth for many years.

By 1865, however, he had gone through most of his savings and returned as an old man to the Little Llano region to retrieve the buried gold and silver. Yet he found the countryside so changed that he couldn't find the tree, the rock, or the spring, much less the buried bullion. He finally gave up, signed on to help drive some cattle to Oklahoma, and was killed in an accident.

In the 1850s a young man named Adam Beasley may have discovered one of the legendary San Saba mines by accident. He was one of several ranchers pursuing some Comanche who had stolen some livestock. While the group was camped, Beasley's horse got loose from the picket line and wandered off. After a two-hour search, Beasley found his mount grazing near a small spring-fed stream at the bottom of a ravine. In one of the ravine walls was a cave. He went exploring and found some old tools and timbers and thick veins of silver in the walls. When he rejoined the hunting party, he kept his secret.

With reports of Comanche in the area, a move to and marriage in Tennessee, and a subsequent return to ranching in Texas, it would be three years before Beasley could search for the cave. He found the pursuit party's campsite on a hilltop easily enough and began to ride out in different directions, confident that he could find the silver mine. Although he searched for almost a week, he never found it. W. C. Jameson speculates that "the San Saba mine, the Bowie mine, and Beasley's silver cave are the same."

Another story tells of a drifter named Medlin, who, in 1878, thirteen years after Perry's return and futile search, worked as a sheepherder for a time on a ranch between the Llano and San Saba rivers. He came upon excavations of some kind and the remains of an old smelter. Nearby were a spring and a pin oak tree with a big rock wedged into a knothole. One version, recorded by Jameson, says that Medlin was "unaware of Perry's treasure cache" and "passed over the area." Then, if he ever did hear about the buried treasure, he apparently could not retrace his steps and find the site.

Another version, passed on by J. Frank Dobie, says that Medlin did know about Perry's buried rods of silver and gold and hired on at the sheep ranch to search for them. In this version, too, he found the markers and spent time digging on the "high hill" Perry had described and around the old smelter. Medlin told a reporter later that somewhere around the ruins he dug up a skeleton of a man with a "miner's spoon"—a soapstone implement used to stir quicksilver into other metals—by his side. Shortly after this discovery, Medlin abandoned his search and headed for South America. Either way, no bullion was unearthed.

A few writers have tried to sort out all these stories. Probably the most comprehensive study of the legends so far is that of C. F. Eckhardt, who spent more than thirty years poring over documents, listening to stories, and tramping through the Texas Hill Country before publishing his findings in 1982. He believes there were and are two mines, the one Miranda discovered and another, also known to the Spaniards, west of the old presidio in present-day Menard. The first he calls Los Almagres, the second Las Iguanas. The latter was mentioned in a report by Teniente Padilla, who visited the presidio in 1810, and by Don Ignacio Obregon, "royal inspector of mines," in 1812. Either or both of these mines could qualify as the Lost San Saba Mine. Neither is the Lost Jim Bowie Mine, in Eckhardt's opinion.

Jim Bowie's acquisition of silver came not from mining, says Eckhardt, but from bullion he took from Spanish mule trains coming up from Mexico. Caravans of up to three hundred mules would carry silver bars from Mexican mines into and sometimes all the way through Texas en route to New Orleans and other locations in the United States. They were generally guarded by fewer than a dozen men, poorly armed. The mule trains could be more than a half-mile long, so it was easy enough, in brushy country with winding trails, to hide out and then cut loose the last three or four mules without being seen. The thieves would then "head for parts unknown with nine hundred to twelve hundred pounds of bar silver."

As evidence of Bowie's propensity for gathering riches from mule trains, both Eckhardt and Robert S. Weddle cite an incident that has come to be known as the "Grass Fight," which occurred shortly before the battle of the Alamo in 1836. Thinking a caravan of Mexican mules would be carrying bags of silver, Bowie led an attack on it in San Antonio. He won the battle but wound up with only bundles of hay being transported to feed Mexican army horses.

So what about the Apache silver mine and the battle on Calf Creek? There were Apache, to be sure, and they may or may not have discovered a silver mine, but it is unlikely that Bowie ever spent time living among them. It is more likely that Bowie simply appropriated a story told by Cephas K. Ham, who had lived with the Indians, albeit Comanche, and who was a survivor of the so-called Calf Creek Fight. Ham was quite a storyteller, apparently, and said that he had been "adopted by the Indians and was— *almost*—shown the mine" the Comanche knew about. One "fat warrior," he said, was a frequent hunting companion and offered to show Ham "plenty of silver" on the other side of a hill, but the band moved on before the two could do any exploring.

According to Dobie, it was Ham who perpetuated the legend that Bowie searched for the Lost San Saba Mine. Again, perhaps believing that truth should never get in the way of a good story, Ham told Colonel John S. "Rip" Ford that Rezin Bowie—Jim's older brother—had already been to the mine and had even hacked off some ore with his tomahawk. When Jim Bowie mounted an expedition to exploit the riches, Ham said, either he could not find the shaft or his attention was diverted by the start of the Texans' war for independence.

Adding to the confusion is an account recorded by J. W. Wilbarger in which Rezin Bowie himself alludes to a trip undertaken by the Bowie brothers and nine others in November 1831 "from San Antonio in search of the old silver mines of the San Saba mission." Of course, it is not likely that Rezin Bowie would announce that the scouting party was, in fact, looking for a silver-laden Mexican pack train. On their way to "the old fort on the San Saba river," the Bowie party was warned by two Comanche and a Mexican that more than 150 Tehuacana, Waco, and Caddo Indians were following and planning an attack. Note that there is no mention of Apache here.

The Bowie party failed to reach the presidio, short by six miles, and looked for "an advantageous place to camp," choosing a spot in a thicket of live oak trees and underbrush near a stream of water. They fortified their encampment by piling up rocks, brush, and dirt. The eleven men, according to Rezin Bowie, fended off 164 Indians over a period of days, with only one man, Thomas McCaslin, killed and three others wounded. The survivors made it back to San Antonio.

The exact location of the Calf Creek Fight is still being debated. Today there are two markers, about thirty miles apart, near Menard, claiming to mark the site. One, erected by the State of Texas in 1936, is 1.3 miles north of Calf Creek in the western edge of McCulloch County on FM 1131. The other was erected on the bank of Silver Creek, a tributary of Dry Creek, twelve miles northwest of Menard on privately owned ranch property. The story behind that marker introduces a colorful pair of latter-day treasure seekers, Judge J. R. Norton and Martha "Princess" Wenonah, granddaughter of a Comanche chief.

Norton, armed with documents he believed were markers and maps obtained from early Spanish records, and Wenonah, relying on information passed down to her, she said, by her Comanche ancestors, teamed up to search for the Lost San Saba Mine. They found a grave. In or near that grave, they found a Bowie knife, an old bridle bit, and an old gun barrel dating back to the 1830s. They believed they had found the grave of Thomas McCaslin, the one casualty out of the Bowie party's battle with the Indians, and planted a large cross made from oil-field pipe. The accompanying metal plaque is inscribed "Here lies Thomas McCaslin who was with the James Bowie expedition and was killed November 21, 1831, in Indian fight in this thicket. Erected by M. Wenonah and J. R. Norton."

According to Weddle, although they "spent many years and eighty thousand dollars looking for the lost mine before her death of cancer in September, 1943, and his a short time later in a stove explosion at his camp on Silver Creek," Wenonah and Norton never found the elusive mine.

Eckhardt argues that both markers are in the wrong place. The state's marker, he says, is nearer to the actual site of the Calf Creek Fight than the other. He contends that the fight more logically took place on the west side of the highway that runs through the community of Calf Creek, "almost exactly opposite the [state's] monument," on a small ranch. He bases his claim on two things: the spring that flows about three-quarters of a mile west of the monument and a grave discovered by the landowner. Rezin Bowie does not mention the name of a creek or spring, but he does describe a "stream of water" near their encampment, and it must have been close enough for the men to reach it quickly while they were under fire. So the spring would satisfy that description. The unearthed grave had been surrounded by an oblong ring of rocks in an area about six feet by three feet. Only human bones—no coffin, weapons, or grave goods of any sort—were discovered. This was more likely "a white man's grave" hastily dug, suggests Eckhardt, whereas the grave at Silver Creek "was arguably an Indian's from the presence of a gun and knife," articles frequently buried with dead warriors.

One last bit of confusion about Jim Bowie's role in any search for the San Saba Mine is the result of an apparent bit of vandalism committed on the gatepost at the San Saba Presidio. Visitors today will find the ruins of the old fort on the Menard Municipal Golf Course. They can still read inscribed into the stone gatepost the name "Bowie" (presumably Jim) and, below that, "Mine" and the date "1832." In notes made during a visit to the presidio in 1846, however, Ferdinand von Roemer recorded that the Bowie inscription carried the date 1829, without any mention of a mine. The original and authentic inscription also included the words *con su tropa* ("and his troops"). The alteration probably dates back to somewhere between 1905 and 1910.

The legend persists. In 1994 a treasure hunter named Frank Buschbacher sought permits to excavate a fifteen-by-fifteen-foot area in front of the Alamo. Why? Because, he claimed, Jim Bowie had made it to the old mission-turned-fortress with a fortune in silver and gold, perhaps the storied San Saba treasure, perhaps silver and gold stolen from Native Americans. According to Buschbacher, Bowie intended to use it to help the Texans finance their revolution, but the Alamo defenders dumped it all in a well when they saw their battle was lost and they were doomed. Buschbacher said that he had learned of the cache from Maria Gomez, a psychic and museum curator in Mexico. Although she had never been to the Alamo, she drew Buschbacher a map indicating where the well was located—originally in what was the Alamo courtyard, now in a street in front of the shrine. Buschbacher got his permits and enlisted the help of the St. Mary's University archaeology department to excavate the site. They found artifacts—"fragments of Native American pottery, the bones of butchered animals, and primitive cooking utensils"—but no silver or gold.

Archaeological surveys and testing are ongoing at the San Saba Presidio as well, most extensively by Texas Tech University. The ruins of the old fort, as seen today, are actually reconstructions undertaken in the 1930s as a Works Progress Administration project and finished in time for the 1936 centennial celebration of Texas's independence from Mexico. Thus far the artifacts found at the site are typical of the Spanish colonial period in Texas: "musket balls, gunflints, horse equipment, hand-forged iron nails, and shards of imported ceramic olive jars, plates, and bowls." Once again, the digs have produced no evidence of gold and silver in the area.

Yet there are two believers, Ed Syers and Charlie Eckhardt, who say they have looked into a mine or mines that could well be the lost ones. Syers reported in 1971 that he was once invited to look into a shaft on a ranch sixteen miles southwest of Llano. The ranch owner had been down in the shaft in the 1940s and had found "old Castilian writing" cut into tunnel walls and "ancient Spanish coins and men's skeletons" in one lateral tunnel. He surmised that this shaft was a ventilation duct and not the main entrance. By the time Syers viewed it, the tunnels had collapsed, and to enter the well-like shaft would have been too dangerous. The location would make it a likely candidate to be the Los Almagres mine.

As for Eckhardt, he says, "I have looked upon the Lost San Saba Mine—two of them—for I have climbed the rough side of Riley Mountain, which is Miranda's Cerro del Almagre, and stared into the hole called the Boyd-Shaft, which is Miranda's Cueva de San Jose del Alcazar, Los Almagres itself, and I have stood in the area known as the Egg-Shaped Basin three leagues west of the old Presidio San Saba and one league north of the river that is the entrance to the still-to-be-reopened Las Iguanas mine." However, neither man saw a vein of gleaming silver. That, it would seem, is still lost.

CHAPTER 3

Return of the Ghost Buffalo

A Kiowa chief named Stone Calf first saw the white buffalo standing alone on a high bluff. Never had Stone Calf seen any buffalo that huge. It was a giant of a beast, and it surveyed all before it with fiery red eyes. Pawing the earth and shaking its great shaggy head, it suddenly turned and disappeared.

Stone Calf climbed the bluff and meant to follow the buffalo, but it was now nowhere in sight. All Stone Calf could find, for all his looking, was the entrance to what appeared to be a large cavern leading underground. There, he thought, must be where the white buffalo went.

In time, others also spotted the strange albino animal. The buffalo hunters, with their powerful Sharps rifles, were eager to kill it as a trophy. And, in time, they did kill a white buffalo. First one, then two, and, finally, seven of the rare animals were killed. Stone Calf heard of this. Yet he continued to see the giant white beast with the fiery red eyes and believed that a great herd was building in the underground cavern. In Stone Calf's mind this growing ghost herd was massing to return one day and reclaim the prairies.

At that time, the buffalo were disappearing. The hunters were slaughtering all they could find, sometimes taking only the hides and leaving the carcasses to rot on the prairies. The once great herds were thinning drastically.

Stone Calf told his story, and it circulated among his people. In his own mind, he began to connect the plight of the buffalo with the plight of the Kiowa. They too were being pushed out of their traditional hunting grounds, just as the buffalo were being killed off on the plains where they grazed. When one returned to power, Stone Calf reasoned, so would the other. This became part of his story, and it too circulated among his people. Someday, Stone Calf said, the herd of white buffalo would emerge from the cavern and take back the land. It would be a day of vengeance, and the ghost animals would haunt those who senselessly killed. On that day the Kiowa nation would rise again.

As if to prove his prediction, another story emerged in the years that followed. No more white buffalo were seen aboveground until one stormy winter day in the Texas Panhandle when a blue norther swept down across the plains. An old hunter, caught out in the storm, finally made it back to camp with a wild story. In the midst of that blizzard, he said, when the wind was blowing the snow almost horizontally, he saw a ghostlike herd of buffalo running at the head of the storm. There must have been millions of them, he said, and they were huge, each one at least six feet tall and weighing a ton or more. Leading the charge was a giant bull, even bigger than the rest, with fiery red eyes. Then the herd just disappeared as if swallowed up by the ground.

How much truth is there to the legend of the white buffalo? According to Ed Syers, folks around Perryton claim that the fabled herd disappeared into the storm right about where Wolf Creek flows into the Canadian River. Syers explored those sandhill breaks himself and could find no caves, but, he says, "When the wind is right and the night makes lightning in the mountains, away west, you can hear something running the long, dark plain."

That there was at least one white buffalo in Texas is easier to prove. On October 7, 1876, on Deep Creek, about ten miles north of present-day Snyder, a buffalo hunter named J. Wright Mooar caught sight of a flash of white in the midst of a buffalo herd. He and another hunter, Dan Dowd, moved on foot through hackberry, chinaberry, and cottonwood trees along the creek and then crawled on their bellies through prairie grass to a place affording a clear shot. Mooar took careful aim and pulled the trigger on his powerful Sharps rifle. The .50-caliber slug hit home, and the white buffalo fell.

It was not a bull with fiery red eyes. It was a four-year-old cow. But it was a rare white buffalo, and it was big. He skinned and butchered it and hung the meat up in a tree until the next morning.

A native of Vermont, Mooar had been a buffalo hunter for three years by the time he came to Texas in 1873 with his brother. He was twenty-five years old when he killed the white buffalo. Over a period of ten years, from 1870 to 1880, Mooar killed an estimated 22,000 animals during what has been called the greatest buffalo hunt—and, perhaps, the worst animal slaughter—in recorded history. Early on, the hunters killed to supply the US Army with meat.

Snyder's white buffalo statue, sculpted by Dr. Robert Taylor, recalls the legendary animal shot near Snyder in 1876.
COURTESY OF THE CITY OF SNYDER, TEXAS

The price per pound ranged from 5 cents to 25 cents. According to an article researched by Mike Cox, during 1876, the year Mooar killed the white buffalo, he sold 62,000 pounds of meat to Fort Griffin, the principal Texas headquarters for the hunters, for 7.5 cents per pound. He made more off the hides: a total of $12,000.

He tanned the prize hide from the white buffalo and kept it until his death (at the age of eighty-nine). Although Teddy Roosevelt once offered $5,000 for it, Mooar refused to sell. Today, one of his descendants still owns the hide.

For many Native Americans, the skin of the white buffalo had magical properties, as the animal itself was believed to have immense power. A warrior wearing such a hide would be protected in battle; a medicine man wearing such a hide would have special healing powers. And a variety of legends about the white buffalo attest to the sacred regard in which the animal was held. According to one tale, the first buffalo, with a thick coat of pure white, came from a cave in the north. It spoke to a nearby Indian: "I and my tribe will come to your people in great numbers. Use us well, for the day will come when we shall disappear back into the earth. And when we are no more, the Indian will soon follow."

The Kiowa, Comanche, and other plains tribes did use the buffalo well and killed only what they needed to survive, using every part of the animal and wasting nothing. As Syers observes, the Texas Panhandle had been "the capital of the buffalo empire— one that lasted a million placid years, then fell before the white hunter in one decade of slaughter—the 1870s." That slaughter was already two years beyond its peak by the time Mooar skinned his white buffalo in 1876, and within the next year or two, the destruction of the four southern buffalo herds that migrated to the Texas Panhandle was largely over.

No longer would herds numbering in the thousands rumble the earth as they roamed across their grazing lands. Sights such as the one rancher Charles Goodnight reported would be no more. He said he once saw the main herd of plains buffalo passing west of present-day Amarillo. It took two days, and he estimated that it was 25 miles wide and 120 miles long. Another pioneer described a herd that he said covered fifty square miles. Yet another swore he saw between two and three million buffalo at one time, and another upped that total to four million. The legendary ghost herd was said to be sixty million strong and would have stretched all the way from Perryton to Abilene.

Among the plains Indians, the Kiowa were not the only ones who told stories about the white buffalo. In fact, O. C. McNary, an acting assistant surgeon in the US Army, in 1885 claimed that Stone Calf's story might be Cheyenne rather than Kiowa. Stationed in Indian Territory, McNary got to know two chiefs he said were Cheyenne well enough to communicate with them in sign language. One of the chiefs was named Stone Calf. McNary recorded that Stone Calf and another chief named Little Robe "were greatly troubled over the disappearance of the buffalo. They told me that the great spirit created the buffalo in a large cave in the Panhandle of Texas; that the evil spirits had closed up the mouth of the cave and the buffalo could not get out. They begged me to get permission from the great father at Washington for them to go and open the cave, and let the buffalo out. They claimed to know the exact location of the cave. They even wanted me to accompany them."

In some tribes the animal was something of a shape-shifter. It could change itself into a white hawk, a gray fox, or even a beautiful woman. The narrative of the white buffalo woman, for example, is central to the mythology of the Lakota, or Sioux, farther north on the Great Plains, but a version of it is claimed by the Kiowa and Apache as well.

This legend is probably even better known than the one about the ghost herd, and all the versions have some key similarities. A woman dressed in white buckskin so polished that it shines floats toward two young warriors who are out scouting for game to feed their starving people. In the Lakota version, she is walking; in the Kiowa version, riding a white buffalo. The two young men approach as the woman and the white buffalo draw near.

In the Lakota version, one of the young men is filled with desire and reaches out to touch the woman. His punishment for disrespecting this holy woman is swift and thorough. Some stories say that lightning instantly strikes him down and leaves nothing but a blackened pile of bones. Others say he is enveloped by a cloud and eaten by snakes that leave only his skeleton.

In both versions of the story, White Buffalo Woman travels to the encampment of the people and teaches them many things as a "culture deity." She brings with her the major ceremonies, customs, and spiritual insights for the tribes, and she gives them a sacred pipe as a representation of the soul of the Earth. In one story, she says, "With this holy pipe, you will walk like a living prayer. Treat this pipe and the earth with respect, and your people will increase and prosper."

She reminds the Kiowa of the Seven Powers and Seven Lights of their True Home and instructs the Lakota in the seven ceremonies symbolized by seven circles carved into a stone. She teaches them about the value of the buffalo, which gives its flesh so that the people might live and not go hungry. She gives the white buffalo to the Kiowa as a symbol of purity.

Promising to return one day, White Buffalo Woman leaves the Lakota by first walking around the circle and then walking away. As the people watch, she rolls over four times and turns into a white buffalo calf. In the Kiowa version, she walks into the moonlight and is swept up by a whirlwind.

From that day forward, the people honored their pipe and performed the seven ceremonies. Buffalo appeared in great herds and allowed themselves to be killed so that the people might survive. So say the legends.

In reality, however, circumstances changed. Once numbering as many as sixty million head, the buffalo herds were brought to the brink of extinction in the late nineteenth century, prompted partly by greed and partly by a strategy to wipe out the herds to eliminate the Indians. After the Civil War, General Philip H. Sheridan became commander of the Department of the Missouri, managing the Indian wars from 1867 to 1883. He is credited with advising the Texans to solve the "Indian question" by taking away both the buffalo and the Indians' horses.

Sheridan wrote in his memoirs:

At the period of which I write, in [winter] 1868, the Plains were covered with vast herds of buffalo—the number has been estimated at 3,000,000 head—and with such means of subsistence as this everywhere at hand, the 6,000 hostiles were wholly unhampered by any problem of food-supply. The savages were rich too according to Indian standards, many a lodge owning from twenty to a hundred ponies; and consciousness of wealth and power, aided by former temporizing, had made them not only confident but defiant.

So, by 1875, Sheridan offered his solution in an address to a joint session of the Texas legislature:

These men [the buffalo hunters] have done more to settle the vexed Indian question than the entire regular army has done in the last thirty years. They are destroying the Indians' commissary. Send them powder and lead if you will, but for the sake of lasting peace let them kill, skin, and sell until the buffalo are exterminated. Then your prairies can be covered with speckled cattle and the festive cowboy who follows the hunter as the second forerunner of an advanced civilization.

By the early twentieth century, only a few hundred buffalo remained in North America, and the Native Americans had little but their legends left to sustain them. They waited for the return of White Buffalo Woman and the white ghost herd. Perhaps that is why, even many years later, such excitement was generated by the birth of a white buffalo calf in Wisconsin in 1994. Named Miracle, she drew thousands of Native American visitors, many of whom saw her birth as a significant prophetic sign.

Miracle's name is indicative of the rarity of a white buffalo's birth. The National Bison Association estimates that the chances are about ten million to one. And Miracle didn't stay white. Her fur turned brown as she matured. Since the stir created by Miracle's birth, a number of other white buffalo calves have been reported, eleven of them on one Arizona ranch alone. So maybe Dr. Richard Spritz, a Wisconsin geneticist specializing in albinism and other pigmentation disorders, is right to dispute the National Bison Association's statistics. Spritz figures that the frequency of albinism in the buffalo population is nearer what it is for humans: about one in 15,000.

Nevertheless, no more white buffalo have been reported in Texas after the one Mooar killed in 1876, one of only seven killed in all of North America. That Texas animal is now memorialized with a statue in downtown Snyder, in the Scurry County courthouse square. Beneath it is a historical marker telling about Mooar. The white buffalo statue is eight feet long and five and a half feet high at the shoulder, as large as some buffalo are in real life. Yet the animal Mooar killed is said to have been bigger.

Ironically, some historians suggest, Mooar and his Kiowa and Comanche adversaries were, in some ways, very much alike. Although Mooar and the other hunters killed buffalo without apology as a business and the Native Americans killed them to survive, they all engaged in a dangerous undertaking requiring courage and skill. No doubt they had a certain degree of respect for one another.

Years after the last of the great buffalo hunts, Mooar and the Comanche chief Quanah Parker talked at a reunion of settlers and Indians about encounters they had in earlier times. Quanah recalled an occasion when he had watched a hunter on the plains near present-day Post in Garza County patiently and deliberately level his rifle at a buffalo a great distance away. Quanah saw smoke when the gun was fired and then saw the buffalo sink, roll, thresh, and die. Amazed at the range of the gun, he returned to his war party to tell them what he had seen.

The hunter was Mooar, who later asked Quanah why he and his Comanche band hadn't returned to attack. "Gun too big," Quanah said. In time Mooar became known among the Native Americans as the man who carried the rifle that "shoots today, kills tomorrow."

Nowadays the only buffalo remaining in Texas are the ordinary dark-brown ones, including the official Texas State Bison Herd, currently at home in Caprock Canyons State Park near Quitaque. And theirs is an intriguing story in itself.

In 1878, the year that spelled the death knell for the southern buffalo herds in Texas, a woman named Mary Ann Goodnight made a request of her husband, Charles. That's the same man who had described once seeing the 120-mile-long herd of buffalo near Amarillo. Mary Ann, whom some called Molly, was haunted by two sounds. By day she heard the ringing of rifle shots. By night she heard the bawling of orphaned calves and realized that she was a witness to the destruction of the native buffalo herds. So she asked Charles to bring some of the calves to their corrals on the ranch. He roped two and brought them home. She began to nurture them, feeding each calf three gallons of milk a day. From that beginning the herd began to grow.

Mary Ann died in 1926 and Charles in 1929. By that time the herd numbered about 250. It passed through several owners after that and eventually, in the 1990s, was given to the State of Texas. In December 1997 Texas park officials began rounding up what is reported to be the purest strain of American bison preserved anywhere and moving them to Caprock Canyons. As it turns out, they are once again, and at long last, roaming a part of their original range. What is now Caprock Canyons State Park was at one time part of the JA Ranch, which was purchased largely with John G. Adair's money but managed in partnership by Charles Goodnight. The buffalo have come home. So maybe there is something after all to the idea that the spirit of the legendary white buffalo lends itself to renewal and regeneration.

CHAPTER 4

The Pacing White Stallion

I magine an old woman named Gretchen sitting in a rocker on the front porch of her Texas Hill Country home. All around her are her grandchildren, perched on the porch rails or sitting on the porch itself. "Tell us a story, Oma," one says. "Yes, tell us about when you first came to Texas," says another. And so she begins:

Oh, way back, when I first came to Texas, there were a whole bunch of us German settlers traveling in wagons along the Guadalupe River. My family was in the last wagon, and we had everything we needed to set up housekeeping. We had beds and bedding, pots and pans, and all the provisions we could carry. Mama had even put in a few potted plants. Then there were all us children, of course.

I must have been eight, going on nine, and Papa always said I was a lively little thing.

We had this old gray mare just a-following along behind the wagon. She was a lazy old thing but just as gentle and loyal as could be. We didn't even have to tie her to the wagon. That's how loyal she was. Oh, she'd stop every now and again to crop a little green grass, but then she'd catch up again. She was a-carrying two big sacks of cornmeal tied on her back. They made kind of a pallet there.

One day I said to Papa, I said, "Papa, can I ride on the old gray mare?" For I did love horses so.

Papa said he didn't see why not, and it might even make for a little more peace and quiet in the back of that wagon. So he lifted me up on the back of the old gray mare, right up on top of those cornmeal sacks. And then he tied me on so as I wouldn't fall off, but still loose enough so's I'd be comfortable. Then we started on down the trail again.

Well, about mid-afternoon one of the wheels on our wagon got wrenched off in a buffalo wallow, and the whole wagon train had to stop while they fixed that wheel. But I didn't know when the wheel got wrenched off or when the wagons stopped because I had fallen asleep. Yessir, I reckon the soft comfort of those cornmeal sacks and the gentle rocking of the old gray mare had just lulled me to sleep.

And I didn't know when the old gray mare kept on grazing down in a little mesquite draw 'til we were plumb out of sight. The folks didn't notice either because they were too busy unloadin' the wagon and gettin' ready to fix that wheel.

I don't know how far we went along there. I reckon what woke me up was that the old gray mare had broken into a gallop. I didn't know she still could. And we were following along behind the most beautiful horse I'd ever seen in my life.

He was white and had a cream-colored mane and tale, and he was prancin' and dancin'. He knew he was pretty.

Oh, I knew I needed to get back to the wagon, but, remember now, I didn't have a rope or a halter, much less a bridle. So I thought maybe I should just jump off and run back to the wagon, but I was tied on. And the knots were all in the back. I couldn't get to them. I was in a fix all right.

About that time we got to a little clearing that was plumb full of horses—mares, I reckon, that belonged to the white stallion. They all came runnin' over to where we were because you know horses are just as cordial as people are. Those mares got to rubbin' noses and nuzzlin' necks and finally got around to where the cornmeal sacks were. They got to nuzzlin' those as well. Some of the cornmeal was coming through the holes in the sacks, I reckon, and those mares got a taste of it. I don't think they'd ever tasted corn before, and they liked it.

So they started nipping at those sacks, and I couldn't get my bare legs out of the way fast enough. Blamed if they didn't start nipping me. I screamed—because it hurt. I thought I was going to be chewed up right there on the spot.

And then the most amazing thing happened. That white stallion was there in a bound, and he ran those mares off. Then—see if you don't think this is smart—he chewed through those ropes that were holding me on, took the collar of my dress in his teeth, and lifted me down off of the old gray mare. He did.

By this time the sun was a-goin' down, and I was missin' my mama and my papa something awful. But Papa had always told me, "If you get lost, stay where you are until you find your-self or someone else finds you." I knew the men would be lookin' for me, but I also knew they weren't very good trackers.

So I made do as best I could. I found a grassy spot under a mesquite tree, tramped that grass down, and settled in my little nest. But I cried myself to sleep that night.

The next morning when I woke up, there wasn't a horse in sight, not even the old gray mare, and I was lonesomer than ever—and hungry. I found me a water hole and got a drink; then I scouted around 'til I came across some wild currants. Those bushes, though, were so thorny and stickery they were pokin' me and scratchin' me, so I didn't eat much.

It was a long day. I picked me some sheep's sorrel for supper, but it's not very good when it's not cooked with some salt pork for greens. When the sun went down and the coyotes started singing their night songs, I crawled back into my nest under the mesquite tree and cried myself to sleep that night too.

The next morning, though, who do you think was stand-ing right there over me? It was the old gray mare, and she must have been plumb tuckered out. She was standing there all stiff-legged like horses do, her ears laid back, sound asleep. But, oh boy, I was glad to see her.

I jumped up, ran down to the water hole, got me a drink, and splashed some water on my face. Then I came back to get on the old gray mare. But she was too tall. I couldn't get up on her. So I took hold of her mane and tried to lead her over to a fallen log I could climb up on. The silly old thing wouldn't budge though. I tried pullin' her; I tried pushin' her; I tried *coaxin' her; I tried throwin' a hissy fit. None of it worked. Finally I put my head on her shoulder and started crying, just bawlin' and squallin'.*

That's when I heard hoofbeats comin' fast behind me. I turned around, and, sure enough, it was that pacing white stallion coming through the brush right toward me. I wasn't a bit scared of him either.

He came up to me, took me by my dress collar again, and lifted me up on the old gray mare. Then I think he told her to just go home because she did. We didn't have any cornmeal left though.

When we got back to the wagons, everybody was still there. The folks weren't goin' anywhere until they found me, and they had been lookin' for me. Like I said, though, they weren't very good trackers. I told them all about my adventures, and they were so glad I was alive and well they didn't even seem to care about the cornmeal.

"Now, you believe that story, don't you?" Gretchen asks her grandchildren. If any of them look as though they don't believe her, she just rolls down her stockings and shows them the faint little scars that are still there from when those mares nipped her legs going after that cornmeal. And then they have to believe her.

Nowadays we'd have to ask ourselves if Gretchen's white stallion could be the same one sighted all the way from Canada to Mexico over a period of fifty-seven years. Or maybe we have to ask whether or not such a white stallion existed at all. Certainly all the reports about him—and there are many—create an intriguing portrait.

A doctor named J. O. Dyer, of Galveston, Texas, is the one who heard and later reported the story of Gretchen's encounter with the pacing white stallion. She was an adult in the 1870s, when she recounted her adventure to him, but she said she had first come to Texas as a young girl in 1848. Years later Dr. Dyer passed her story on to J. Frank Dobie, and Dobie included it in a whole catalog of tales about the legendary mustang, first published in 1934.

In each account, the wild horse is distinctive for two reasons: its color and its gait. A white horse among the herds of mostly black and brown horses running across the prairies would be rare enough, but one that paced rather than trotted or galloped was doubly unique. A pace is distinguished from a trot in that the pacing horse lifts the front and back legs on the same side and rocks from side to side as it moves forward; a trotting horse lifts right front–left rear and left front–right rear together, making for a more even gait for both horse and rider, if there is a rider. In none of the stories about the pacing white stallion is it ever ridden.

Pacing is faster than trotting, and the white stallion was noted for exceptional speed. One of the earliest descriptions of the legendary steed was recorded by George W. Kendall in 1842 and quoted by Dobie. Although Kendall never claimed to see the horse himself, he heard tales about it in camps on the Staked Plains of Texas. According to Kendall, "Some of the hunters go so far as to say that the White Steed has been known to pace his mile in less than two minutes." That is entirely possible, as racing pacers have been clocked at under two minutes per mile, even while pulling a sulky. The famous Dan Patch's record of 1:55:25, set in 1903, was

Tom Lea's painting of the pacing white stallion was inspired by legends about the elusive mustang.
HARRY RANSOM HUMANITIES RESEARCH CENTER, THE UNIVERSITY OF TEXAS AT AUSTIN

broken in 1960 by Adios Butler, with a time of 1:54:03. Neither of those horses, however, was white.

Dobie says he spent thirty years tracking the white stallion in folktales and literature, and his citations have provided the basic bibliography for every researcher on the topic since. The earliest mention he found was in Washington Irving's *A Tour of the Prairies*. In the fall of 1832, Irving heard several anecdotes, he said, about a famous horse, actually gray rather than white, that roamed the prairies in present-day Oklahoma. It reportedly could pace "faster than the fleetest horse can run." The stories Kendall later heard placed the horse in the Cross Timbers region near the Red River, either in Oklahoma or across the river in Texas.

About the same time as Kendall's narratives, Josiah Gregg's reports on his trip west over the Santa Fe Trail appeared. He too heard "marvelous tales" about a mustang stallion that was "milk-white, save for a pair of black ears, a natural pacer." The stories Gregg collected had the horse at times in the northern Rocky Mountains, on the Arkansas River, and on the borders of Texas, thereby broadening the range somewhat. Another chronicler quoted by Dobie, François des Montaignes, wrote about an exploratory expedition in 1845. He mentions the "celebrated snow-white pacer of the Canadian," a river that flows through part of New Mexico, across the Texas Panhandle, and into Oklahoma. This horse, Montaignes says, might be visible "only to special and favorite individuals."

It was Herman Melville who gave the pacing white stallion real literary stature by mentioning the horse in *Moby Dick*. In the chapter on "The Whiteness of the Whale," Melville includes "the White Steed of the Prairies" in his list of the white objects of the earth. He describes the horse as "a magnificent milk-white charger, large-eyed, small-headed, bluff-chested, and with the dignity of a thousand monarchs in his lofty, over-scorning carriage."

A writer named Mayne Reid picked up Melville's label of the White Steed of the Prairies and placed the stallion, or at least the stories about him, "throughout all the wild borders of prairie-land." Like Gregg, Reid claimed that the horse had distinctive markings: "His ears were black—only his ears, and these were the color of ebony. The rest of his body, mane and tail, were white as fresh-fallen snow."

Meanwhile, tales about the white stallion emerged as well from central Texas, where Gretchen's story is set. Dobie notes that John W. Young, a rancher on Onion Creek in the 1840s, near

Austin, reported seeing "an extraordinary stallion" watering with other mustangs at Onion Creek. "He was pure white," and his "only gait out of a walk was a pace." He was seen crossing the Guadalupe River, along which Gretchen's family traveled, and moved as far south as the Nueces River. It is this horse whose fate is known, if the stories are to be believed.

Many men tried to capture the horse, but, in most accounts, the white stallion manages through speed or cunning to evade riders, ropers, and snares. Finally, however, he was caught, according to a story Dobie heard from John R. Morgan, a nephew of Young's. After leading a long chase toward the Rio Grande, the white stallion had foiled the efforts of a dozen vaqueros to catch him, but he was thirsty and tired. As he emerged from a water hole in a box canyon, weighted down with the water he had just drunk, yet another vaquero on a fresh pony gave chase and managed to rope the stallion. Although the white pacer put up quite a fight, he was finally snubbed, tied, and staked on a grassy spot with water provided in a trough. There he remained for ten days and ten nights, refusing to eat or drink, until he simply lay down and died rather than submit to captivity.

No date has been specified for the possible demise of the white stallion, but it would have been before 1868, when Morgan began to work for his uncle and heard the stories, and at least late in the 1840s or in the 1850s after the last reported sightings in central Texas. So the time and place would be right to make it possible for this horse to be the same one Gretchen encountered in 1848.

But there would have had to have been two—or more—pacing white stallions to account for simultaneous appearances on the prairies of Oklahoma and northern Texas and in the hills and along the river valleys in central and south Texas. Moreover, it's doubtful that one horse, and a wild one at that, could live fifty-plus years, say the skeptics. The average life span for a domesticated horse is twenty to thirty years, and for a wild horse only fifteen to eighteen. Remember that Irving said he heard about the white stallion in 1832. One of the last claimed sightings came from a man who said he saw the horse near Phoenix, Arizona, in 1889, fifty-seven years later. That story, like Morgan's, ended with the horse's capture, its refusal to eat or drink in captivity, and its death.

Countless other stories, of course, have been passed down orally by Native Americans and other frontiersmen coming into Texas in the nineteenth century. Both Indian lore and some cowboy lore refer to a "ghost horse," and in some of the tales the pacing white stallion is called the "winged steed" or "Wind Drinker." These designations speak to the mythic and even supernatural qualities assigned to the horse over the years as his legend grew and spread. He was viewed by many Native Americans as a spirit horse rather than as a living, breathing animal and, as such, one that could not be killed or injured. In Texas, the Kiowa, in particular, believed that neither prairie fire nor hunters' bullets could harm him. These days "ghost wind stallions" are said to be possible descendants of the ghost horse and are the sires of the Appaloosa breed, with its distinctive spotted patterns, generally over a white background, on the hips or along more extended parts of the body.

Only about 50,000 mustangs of any color remain in the wild today, and that may be too many for the available range. Since 1971 the Bureau of Land Management has maintained and managed wild horses and burros in the United States in 270 "herd management areas" totaling about thirty-five million acres in ten states. Texas is not one of those states. Each mustang herd numbers between 135 and 180 adult horses, and the ideal manageable total, according to the Bureau of Land Management, should be no more than 26,600, a far cry from the estimated two million that once ran free. Today's herds roam public lands in Arizona, California, Colorado, Idaho, Montana, Nevada, New Mexico, Oregon, Utah, and Wyoming.

Gone are the days when rewards were offered for the capture of prize specimens like the pacing white stallion (P. T. Barnum is said to have offered a reward of $5,000 for the horse), and there are criminal penalties for "removing, converting to private use, killing, harassing, selling, or processing the remains of wild horses and burros under federal jurisdiction without federal authority." In fact, only the Bureau of Land Management is now authorized to conduct periodic round-ups and then offer adoptions out of the pool of captured horses. Some of those adopted animals live now in Texas, but none roam free.

The 1971 act preserving wild horses and burros on federal lands protects them as "living symbols of the historic and pioneer spirit of the West," but none is ever again likely to be so noteworthy and enduring, at least in Texas, as the legendary pacing white stallion.

CHAPTER 5

Bigfoot in Texas

As a southeast Texas woman's car lights swept along the edge of a creek in Jackson County one night in the fall of 2000, she saw it again, illuminated in the headlights: a great hairy creature probably seven and a half or eight feet tall. It put up its hand as if to block the light from its eyes. She sped past and recalled another encounter only about a week earlier.

Actually, it all started about two weeks earlier with a call from her brother, who lived across the street. He said he had heard his dogs barking out toward the pasture and had gone to investigate, carrying a flashlight. He swung the beam on an old vehicle he had in the pasture and saw eyes. While he was trying to figure out what he was looking at, something turned and ran. It scared him so much, he said, that he beat the dogs back to the house. "It ran your direction," he told his sister.

At first, she and her family just laughed the story off, asking the brother if he had been drinking. Nevertheless, her husband went outside to look around but saw nothing.

Then one evening, about a week after that, she flipped on the porch light and went outside to throw something in the trash. She had her back to the pasture, when all of a sudden she got a funny feeling that someone or something was staring at her. She turned around, and there it was, slumped over next to her husband's pickup, its arms dangling. The creature was staring at her with glowing red eyes.

In a panic, she ran for the house, shaking and crying, "It's out there!"

"Mom, what is it?" her daughter asked.

"Your uncle wasn't lying; that thing is out there."

Once again, her husband hurried to the porch, but the creature had run off. Later the family determined that it had been bedding down in an old hog pen but spent most of its time in the woods not far from the creek. The creek is not far from the Lavaca River, which runs parallel to the Navidad River.

When she told her story later, the woman said, "We have them down here—Sasquatch, Bigfoot, whatever you want to call it. I'm living proof." For years, she said, there have been reported sightings of similar creatures that the locals refer to as the "Navidad Wildman." And that calls for another story, or maybe two.

More than 170 years ago, settlers along the lower Navidad first reported seeing tracks of what they assumed were two barefooted human beings. The size of the tracks led them to believe that one set was made by a boy, the other by a girl or a small woman. At first, the mysterious pair invaded only the sweet potato fields or the corn patches during the night, and they didn't harvest much—only enough to eat.

Among the theories offered were that they were runaway slaves or Indians or lost children separated from their parents following the fall of the Alamo in 1836. No one ever saw the makers of the tracks.

Then, after some years, only one set of tracks appeared, the smaller set. Before long, some hunters said they had come across a crude burial site, just some bones sticking out of a pile of sticks and leaves. They uncovered a human skeleton and supposed that it must be the remains of the larger of the two reclusive night visitors. And still the surviving track maker came to the sweet potato fields. Residents in the area began to call her—for they assumed it was a female who remained—the "wild woman" or, simply, "it" or "that thing that comes."

Then the wild woman became bolder and began entering houses to take things. Most of the settlers' houses were built on the "dog trot" model, with a covered, central, open hallway separating two enclosed living areas, the better to catch breezes during hot Texas summers. Doors and windows were often left open, but every household had vigilant, and sometimes vicious, dogs to sound an alarm or go after unwanted visitors. Yet the dogs never so much as whimpered when the wild woman entered, necessarily stepping over them, and made her way to open cupboards to take bread, meat, milk, butter, or whatever else might be left out. But she never took more than half.

Long periods might pass without a sign of her, and then she would show up—or, at least, evidence of her presence would appear. At one point, some woodworking tools disappeared from an open shed on one of the plantations. The owner missed a handsaw, a drawing knife, and some other tools, but only for a few weeks. They were all returned to their original places, and the handsaw was scoured and polished brighter than new. Later a neighbor missed a log chain, twelve feet long and heavy, weighing thirty pounds or more. It too was returned scoured and polished.

For seven years the wild woman moved like a spirit in and out of fields and houses and sheds without once being announced by dogs or caught by the men who sometimes hid and waited.

Her next exchange was a hog for a hog. She took a fattening hog from a farmer's pen and left in its stead a poor substitute from the woods. Neither the farm dogs nor the two hogs made a sound. People began to say she put a spell on the animals.

Hunters occasionally came across what they supposed was one of her camps. She had made a bed of moss and leaves, but there were no signs of a fire, no implements, and no clothing. There might be a pile of sugarcane taken from neighboring fields, cut into short lengths, and chewed. A long time passed, and then another camp was found some distance from the earlier one. This time handmade baskets and what appeared to be a snare were found, as well as articles taken from houses: a spoon; some table knives; a cup; several books, including a Bible; and an old letter. So could she read? Just in case, serious hunters posted letters to the wild woman on trees. None was ever touched.

Meanwhile, a man named Samuel C. A. Rogers had his own adventures with the wild people, and he later recorded them and passed them on.

Sam was not a wealthy man, by any means. In fact, he had no money in his pocket at all. But he did have a little place of his own near Sandy Creek in southeast Texas on which he raised some cattle and corn and sweet potatoes. He and his wife, Lucinda, had a little boy named John. Others in the household were a hired hand by the name of Hall and another fellow named Franklin Rogers.

Then, in the spring of 1845, Sam saw signs that there might be three more people in the neighborhood. Going to work one morning, he came across some tracks near his house. They were fresh, made the night before. The smallest was a barefoot track that Sam judged to be about a size four; the second set was larger and showed one foot bare and one foot shod; the third set was larger still, maybe size nine or ten. Whoever made the tracks had done no mischief that he could see, but there was cause for wonder.

About this same time, Lucinda was hankering for a new calico dress, and Sam wanted a fishing seine. Fishing was pretty good in the Sandy and in the nearby Navidad River, but it was slow with only a line and a pole. Sam figured he could haul out more fish with a seine. So he struck a bargain with Lucinda. If she would use her spinning wheel to spin enough cotton thread for the fishing seine, he would buy her the calico for her dress. Every evening after the housework was done, she worked on the spinning. In time the thread was spun and the seine was tied. Sam had to sell off eight cowhides at $1 apiece to raise the money to buy Lucinda's calico, but it was worth it. He was netting fish by the bucket loads.

Then one morning Sam and Franklin went to check the seine and found it cut and half gone. They saw the tracks, prompting a surprising outburst from Franklin: "Them wild people. If we can't catch or kill them, they will break us up." Almost two weeks later, the hired hand began cursing the wild people too, claiming they had taken one of his trace chains so that he couldn't plow. After that it was potatoes missing from the potato patch.

By this time the wild people had been taking things and leaving tracks around Sam's place for almost a year. But then only one set of tracks remained. The big ones and the little ones were gone. And still Sam had not seen hide nor hair of the creatures that made them.

The one wild man—or wild woman—who was left came in nearly every night to harvest a few roasting ears out of Sam's corn patch, and one morning Sam missed a handsaw he had left out in the yard. Over the next two years, the wild one even entered Sam's house, taking away one of Sam's shirts, a novel, a Bible, and a number of other articles.

Finally, two brothers named Ward surprised what they took to be a wild man in the river bottom and retrieved a basket he dropped. In it, among other things, were Sam's shirt, the novel, and the Bible. The men found the handsaw too. Encouraged by the sighting, one of the Wards proposed that all the neighbors gather to hunt down what they had now decided was a wild man.

Eight men, Sam among them, collected where the Sandy flows into the Navidad. An all-day search produced nothing, although later the men found two trees in which the wild man had lived or taken refuge when the river would rise. Sam climbed up in the big live oak that forked about thirty feet above ground and found the flat place where the wild man could lie down and sleep. There was even a place where he could build a fire, if he knew how and had a mind to.

That's as close as Sam got, though, to ever seeing the mysterious visitor.

So what did happen to the wild man or the wild woman? No one was yet sure about the gender.

Eventually, a number of hunters came up with a plan for men with hounds to flush the wild one out of a wooded area it frequented into a small prairie clearing, where mounted men with lassos would be waiting. The plan worked, up to a point. What the men now perceived to be the wild woman burst onto the prairie, running hard for the woods on the other side of the clearing. The riders spurred their horses and shook out their loops. The horses, however, began to shy away from the strange creature, so the loops missed their target. The men were left with only a fleeting image and a club the wild one had dropped. It was about five feet long and polished to a sheen never before seen by any of them. And they now had a description of what they still thought was a woman, naked except for a covering of short brown hair.

More time passed with no more sign of the wild one. Then, during the severe winter of 1850, hunters came across a camp in the brush of a fallen tree. There was no evidence of a fire, but they found a bed made with moss and leaves; several piles of cut sugar-cane, some of it chewed; the strange snares; and tracks in the snow. Spring came, and fresh signs appeared. The men mustered again with hounds and horses. This time they closed in from all sides, and the wild one climbed a tree, looking down in fright at the men and the baying hounds.

The wild one turned out to be a man, a small African American who would not or could not communicate with his captors. The full story emerged only when a wandering sailor came along who had spent time in Africa and knew something of the captive's tribe and language. According to the wild man, he had been sold as a boy by his parents to slave traders and brought to this country in a ship. In time he and others were brought to a river and kept in a large house on a plantation where there was plenty of sugarcane. He and another slave, a grown man from his tribe, had escaped and wandered through woods and across rivers and prairies until they reached the area around the Navidad River, and there they stayed. The other man died after several years and left this man to survive as best he could.

The little man seemed to know, the sailor explained, that time of night when a dog is in its deepest sleep and not likely to be roused, but the techniques for burnishing tools and swapping hogs remained unsolved mysteries.

And now the question remains: Could those early small-footed wild ones have big-footed descendants still roaming in the Texas woods? Not likely, according to the Texas Bigfoot Research Conservancy (TBRC), formed in 1999 to "investigate and conduct research regarding the existence of the unlisted primate species known as the sasquatch or bigfoot." The TBRC operates on the premise that the sasquatch/bigfoot (the term *bigfoot* came into being only as recently as 1958) is more nearly akin to a gorilla than to a human. Although the sasquatch may at first seem humanlike, says the TBRC website, "there are several aspects of its appearance that differ from the human form."

First, there is the matter of size—large to the point of massiveness, with very broad shoulders and a thick chest—and shape. Whatever neck exists is "very thick and maybe short," as one young man reported after coming "face to face with a sasquatch near Jefferson, Texas, in 1989." A female motorist described a sasquatch she witnessed in Newton County in 1986 as having a "flat" face. Then there's the hair. Generally, at least in Texas, the sasquatch is described as having black or dark hair, or sometimes reddish-brown hair. The young man near Jefferson said the animal he saw had hair that appeared "dull and coarse." It "covered most of the body, not including the face (with the exception of the cheeks and jawline), forehead, palms of hands," and the hair was thinner on the chest and abdominal areas.

Furthermore, the greatest number of reported sightings nowadays comes not from the southeastern Gulf coast area where the Navidad River flows but from the East Texas Piney Woods. In fact, the Jackson County woman's account of her two encounters with the sasquatch creature is the only one reported to the TBRC from the Navidad area. By contrast, three counties in the Piney Woods had more than ten reported sightings each. Montgomery County, north of Houston, had the most, with thirteen. More than 47,000 acres in that county form part of the Sam Houston National Forest, which "may well have the highest concentration of reported sightings in the four-state [Texas, Oklahoma, Arkansas, and Louisiana] area," according to Daryl Colyer, cofounder of the TBRC and seasoned outdoorsman with a background in US Air Force intelligence. Colyer investigates many of the reports that come into the TBRC by interviewing the witnesses who describe their encounters and by visiting sites where the alleged sightings took place.

So has Colyer ever seen a sasquatch himself? Yes, he believes he has, in May 2004 on a trail near the Trinity River in Liberty

County. As he told Craig Woolheater, another cofounder of the TBRC and current chair of the board who investigated his report, it was just before sunset when Colyer and his wife were returning home after a baseball game. They crossed the Trinity River on Highway 105 and turned off on a dirt road to investigate a waterfall in a small creek off the Trinity on the east side of the river. As they walked down a two-track trail, Colyer saw "an upright reddish-brown large animal" leap across the trail about forty yards ahead. It looked similar to an orangutan but was much larger, he said. He estimated that it was about six feet tall and that it leapt about ten feet. His wife was preoccupied and did not see the creature, but they both ran to the spot where the animal crossed. They found no tracks but said they could hear the animal "still running in the woods." Colyer said he smelled a musky odor similar to that of a horse. They theorized that the sasquatch had been watching, from the cover of the trees, a group of people playing and listening to music on a sandbar on the other side of the river. There was also evidence that the creature might have been building some kind of crude shelter, as several trees had been uprooted.

Woolheater, by the way, says he encountered a sasquatch himself "somewhere in the swampy woods near Alexandria, Louisiana," in 1994. In that area the creature is sometimes called a "woolly booger." Woolheater says that most people "think that Bigfoot is a Pacific Northwest phenomenon," but, he points out, Texas has twenty-two million acres of forestland. Furthermore, he adds, "there have been sightings in every state of the Union except Hawaii."

The Texas Bigfoot reportedly prefers a wooded habitat like this in Harrison County. PAUL PORTER, PHOTOGRAPHER

Skeptics, of course, want evidence, preferably a sasquatch captured, dead or alive, and on display. They're not satisfied with eyewitness reports, plaster casts of huge footprints, or photographs or film footage that could, they say, be part of a hoax. But serious scientists like Grover S. Krantz, an anthropologist; Loren Coleman, who calls himself a cryptozoologist, one who studies "hidden animals"; and Jane Goodall, famous for her studies on chimpanzees and other primates, have argued that ongoing research is legitimate and vital. Dr. Krantz made a serious study of the sasquatch and estimated that its life span is about forty years. He was not opposed to the idea of killing a bigfoot to prove they exist, but hunters have apparently not been willing or able to fire on one, as one Texas man observed. Although he was armed as he hunted along the San Jacinto River bottom in Montgomery County, he did not fire at the sasquatch that he said he saw "come out of the swamp area."

For one thing he was too startled; for another he was reluctant to shoot something he could not identify. Truly, he said, "I am glad I did not shoot this animal. It was just that—an animal. I had a .45 side arm and a Bushmaster AR rifle with me—a kill shot could have been made, but this was something I could not kill."

As to why no remains of a sasquatch have been found in the wild, Coleman says, "Porcupines and rodents eat the bones of dead animals. And most dying animals hide themselves in caves and other quiet places when they feel sick—and then die. We are not surprised we haven't found any Bigfoot bones." Yet people are still looking. Dr. Goodall, appearing on National Public Radio's *Talk of the Nation: Science Friday* in September 2002, told host Ira Flatow, "You'll be amazed when I tell you that I'm sure that they [large 'undiscovered' primates such as sasquatch] exist." She added, "Of course, the big, big criticism of all this is, 'Where is the body?' You know, why isn't there a body? I can't answer that, and maybe they don't exist, but I want them to."

The idea that a sasquatch does exist is so fascinating to people that a special bigfoot exhibit at the Institute of Texan Cultures in 2006 became a great success. Woolheater, of the TBRC, helped organize the exhibit, which included a re-creation of an east Texas thicket and ran for almost four months. The institute, located in San Antonio, took no position on whether a Texas bigfoot exists, but Willie Mendez, project director for the exhibit, said that the TBRC organizers seemed to be "really credible people." Visitors to the exhibit were given a chance to vote on whether they believed the evidence was convincing. On the first day, at least, "yeas outweighed nays 178 to 53."

CHAPTER 6

Chasing Chupacabras

When something started raiding Phylis B. Canion's chicken pen, her hunter's instinct kicked in, and she set out to catch the varmint. She rigged up a video camera and right away saw that a bobcat came in the night and carried away one of her chickens. She killed the bobcat.

Then she began to find some of her chickens dead in their cages, meat and feathers still on the bone, but the carcasses apparently bled out. That mystery was not so easily solved, and no more images showed up on the video. Meanwhile, she and some of the other ranchers around Cuero, a town about eighty miles southeast of San Antonio, caught occasional glimpses of a strange doglike animal in the area. For two years she watched the creature roam the vicinity, and she counted her losses in the chicken yard: during that time, a total of twenty-six chickens were left dead but uneaten.

A car finally did what the ranchers could not or, at least, did not do, and one of the strange animals wound up as roadkill near the entrance to the Canions' ranch. With the dead body in her

60

possession, Canion—her friends call her Phyl—was more curious than queasy as she decided to skin the creature and keep its head for further examination. First of all, though, she took pictures. The animal was about the size of a coyote but hairless except for a little fuzz down its back; it had blue eyes and bluish skin, and its front legs were shorter than the back ones by about two inches. It had big ears, a long snout, two large upper canine incisors, and two worn lower incisors.

The Associated Press heard about the find and interviewed Canion. "It is one ugly creature," she said. "I've seen a lot of nasty stuff. I've never seen anything like this." She decided it just might be a chupacabra, a legendary blood-sucking beast first reported in Puerto Rico and then in Mexico. That caught the AP's attention, and newspapers and television broadcasts across the country picked up the story and accompanying photos and videoed interviews.

Could it be that chupacabras really do exist and that this Texas woman now had one stowed in her freezer?

A veterinarian from nearby Victoria looked at the evidence. "I'm not going to tell you that's not a chupacabra. I just think in my opinion a chupacabra is a dog." But a blood-sucking dog? Unusual, yes, the vet agreed, but it's possible that this kind of dog prefers its prey to bleed out before it feeds by licking up the blood. Maybe it's just some new kind of mutt or part of a mutated litter of dogs, he opined. A south Texas game warden, even without seeing the beast, said, "I'd put my money on it being a mangy coyote." The state mammalogist agreed with the mange theory, but he thought the animal was a gray fox. "When mange goes untreated it causes this type of reaction," he said. "They start to itch, lose all their hair, blue gray coloration, and the animal usually dies from it." If a car doesn't hit it first, that is.

Canion and her ranching neighbors weren't entirely satisfied with those answers. "There have been so many stories for so long," Canion said. "The chupacabra is a mythical thing [people say] and maybe it is, but this is something . . . a cross between something. What? I don't know; I'd love to find out." So she sent tissue samples off to Texas State University for DNA testing. The results came back saying that the DNA was similar to that of a coyote. Canion wanted a second opinion. "It just didn't have features of any animal I have ever seen," she said. She sent more tissue samples off, this time to the University of California at Davis. And this time the results were a little more detailed. On the maternal side the creature's ancestry did appear to be coyote. On the paternal side, however, the Y chromosome matched that of the Mexican wolf. So perhaps it's a hybrid. "I think it could have wolf in it," Canion said. "It has to be a cross between two or three different things."

But the Mexican wolf is not all that common in Texas. A reduction in its natural prey, like deer and elk, had led the Mexican wolf to attack domestic livestock, so government agencies sanctioned removal efforts. By the 1950s hunters and trappers, and others determined to eradicate it, eliminated it from the wild. As a result, although this relative of the gray wolf is native to North America, it is now the "rarest and most genetically distinct subspecies." It is considered to be "endangered" and survives mostly in captivity in zoos and other wildlife facilities. Recent efforts to reintroduce the animal into the wild are not centered in Texas.

Whatever the mystery animal's genetic makeup and origins, its presence created quite a stir in Cuero. Canion and her neighbors, during a four-day period in July 2007, discovered the bodies of three such animals—all roadkill victims.

Canion's theory is that heavy rains ran the creatures "right out of their dens" and that a cataract condition impaired their vision enough to make them susceptible victims on the road. DNA testing on a second one showed that it too "had DNA similar to that of a coyote." Canion continues to make the point that "similar" or "almost" does not make the DNA a match. She says the test results she secured also rule out another theory that the creatures in question are Mexican hairless dogs, a rare breed also known as *xoloitzcuintli,* or xolo, for short. As its name implies, the xolo is hairless as a result of "a spontaneous mutation thousands of years ago," and the color of its skin is generally black or blue. Owners and breeders think it is extremely unlikely that a pack of feral xolos would be running loose in south Texas.

So is the Cuero creature a hybrid, a mutant, a new subspecies? Maybe. But for now its status as a chupacabra is generally cataloged as cryptid, a creature whose existence has been suggested but is not yet validated with scientific proof. There is no lack of lore, however, about the legendary chupacabra. The term derives from the Spanish words *chupar* ("to suck") and *cabra* ("goat"), suggesting both method and preferred victim. Chupacabras have also developed a taste for the blood of smaller animals, like cats, dogs, and barnyard fowl, if all the stories are to be believed.

Although some argue that such a beast has been around for more than fifty years, recorded stories about the chupacabra first began to circulate in Puerto Rico in the late 1980s and described "a stealthy beast that sucked the blood of goats." In 1987 two Puerto Rican newspapers, *El Vocero* and *El Nuevo Día,* reported numerous livestock deaths, noting that the animals' blood had been drained through circular incisions in their flesh. Generally there were two puncture wounds in the neck, although some reports mentioned only one or even three puncture wounds, some of them occurring in the chest area. The deaths and the stories then spread throughout Central and South America. A Puerto Rican comedian, Silverio Perez, coined the term *chupacabras*, and the name stuck.

Early descriptions of the chupacabra tended more toward the reptilian than the canine. It was said to be lizard-like, with "leathery/scaly greenish-gray skin" and dinosaur-like sharp spines or quills down its back. Its head and face, however, appeared more like that of a dog or a panther, even though it still had a reptile's forked tongue and large fangs. It was said to hiss and to screech, and it had a "sulfuric stench." Generally bipedal, it hopped like a kangaroo, covering as much as twenty feet at a jump. Early drawings give it an appearance similar to that of a medieval gargoyle.

In a variant on that version of the chupacabra, it is still standing and hopping like a kangaroo, but it is no longer hairless. In fact, it is described as having "coarse fur" and "grayish facial hair." Again, its head is similar to that of a dog, and it has "large teeth." Some of the early descriptions included details such as "glowing red eyes," a "bulbous head," and "bat-like wings." A common belief was that the chupacabra's eyes had the power to hypnotize or paralyze its prey.

Theories about where the animals came from ran the gamut from claims that they were an entirely new species—possibly the

A Blanco, Texas, taxidermist created this mount of an alleged chupacabra.
© LostWorldMuseum.com

result of some genetic experiment gone awry—to their being extra-terrestrial alien pets that escaped from or got left behind by a space ship. The one thing that remained constant was their vampire-like attacks and propensity to feed on the blood of other animals.

As reports of the chupacabra's physiology and supposed origin moved from country to country, other variants emerged, and, by the time it got to Texas, the creature appeared to be some sort of wild dog. Gone were the membrane-like wings, the forked tongue, and the red eyes, although it was described as having "pronounced eye sockets" and bigger-than-usual teeth and claws. Sometimes it was said to stand erect, but generally it ran on all fours. It had a "pronounced spinal ridge" but no actual spines or quills. Mostly hairless, it was said to weigh about forty pounds and be no more than three or four feet tall. Less dramatic speculation about this chupacabra's origins tends more toward some sort of inbreeding, mutation, or hybridization.

Meanwhile, chupacabra sightings have now been reported as far north as Maine and as far south as Chile. In recent years, reports have come from Russia and from the island of Maui in Hawaii. But the longest list may come from Texas.

Even before the roadkill trio in Cuero, a rancher near San Antonio killed a hairless, doglike creature he said had been attacking livestock. This was in July 2004. Dubbed the Elmendorf Beast, it was ultimately determined to be "an unknown canine of some sort, similar to a coyote with demodectic mange." By October of the same year, two more animals matching the description of the Elmendorf Beast were found dead in the same area. Biologists studied those specimens and agreed that the animals were "some sort of canines of an undetermined species." Also in 2004 a resident of the east Texas town of Lufkin shot and killed a similar unidentified creature as it tried to crawl under his house.

In 2006 a farmer, Reggie Lagow, in Coleman, set a trap to catch whatever had been killing his chickens and turkeys. What he caught, Lagow said, looked like "a mix between a hairless dog, a rat, and a kangaroo." He turned it over to Texas Parks and Wildlife, but it apparently got thrown out with the trash, he said.

Then 2007 became the summer of the chupacabra in Cuero, and there were even T-shirts to announce and celebrate the fact. Phyl Canion says it started as a sort of family joke: a T-shirt sporting a caricature of the chupacabra and the slogan "2007, The Summer of the Chupacabra, Cuero, Texas." The T-shirts sold at cost for $5 apiece, and the demand grew. Within a year "nearly 10,000 people across the United States and 21 countries" owned the T-shirts, Canion told a San Antonio television reporter. She kept them inexpensive, she said, "because I want everybody who can to have one and help to show that the chupacabra is from the area of Cuero." She's still selling T-shirts, but now they're updated to say "I would rather be in Cuero, Texas, looking for a Chupacabra." Total sales are upwards of 30,000. She sees her efforts as a possible boost to tourism as well as an entrepreneurial opportunity. "If everyone has a fun time with it, we'll keep doing it. It's good for Cuero." And she bristles at the suggestion that she's cashing in on her notoriety. "I'm happy to get a little recognition for Cuero, but this is not about money."

She is still quite eager to prove that chupacabras do exist, and she honestly believes she had "the mother and one other one" to study. Already the author of *The A B C's of Nutrition* (she is a nutritionist), she is now writing a book about the Cuero chupacabras. As long as people are intrigued by the mystery of the chupacabra cryptids, she plans to continue her quest.

Adding credence to the claim of chupacabras in the Cuero area is a deputy's video footage of an unidentified animal running down one of the back roads in DeWitt County. Brandon Riedel and his partner were patrolling in a remote area when they saw the animal and turned on the dashboard camera as they followed it in August 2008, a little more than a year after Canion and her neighbors gathered up the roadkill specimens. "You need to record something like this because it's not every day you find something that looks like this running around out in the middle of the county," Riedel said. The creature Riedel filmed was "about the size of a coyote but was hairless with a long snout, short front legs, and long back legs." The deputy's boss, County Sheriff Jode Zavesky, figures that it may be the same species identified by Texas State University from the DNA submitted by Canion in 2007. "You know, it's just kind of one of those things to hear about and talk about, but to actually see something on video that may actually be a live one, that's pretty amazing," Zavesky said.

In the spring and summer of 2009, reports of chupacabra sightings in south Texas continued to come in. A San Antonio resident e-mailed a local television station in March 2009 to say he had seen a mysterious four-legged animal that might be a chupacabra on the city's northwest side. It had been struck by a car going about 40 miles per hour, he said, and seemed dazed and confused before it "popped up and darted away."

In August 2009 Jerry Ayer, a taxidermist and teacher at Blanco Taxidermy School, appeared on CNN and other broadcast outlets with news that he had the body of what some believed might be a chupacabra. One of his students brought it in, he said. The animal had died farther south in Rosenberg, near Houston, not in Blanco. It had, in fact, been poisoned by the student's cousin. "It got into his cousin's barn, and they thought maybe it was a rodent tearing things up, and they had no idea since they've never seen it. He got out some poison, and this is what they got the very next day," Ayer said. The animal, preserved as a frozen carcass, was a gray, hairless, leathery, long-legged beast with large fangs. "Different, that's for sure," said Ayer, "very interesting." As a ten-year veteran in the taxidermy business, Ayer said he has never seen anything like it. "The front legs seem to be a little bit longer than a typical coyote, very irregular." That's a departure from other descriptions of creatures with their front legs shorter than their back legs. Otherwise, the characteristics are similar. Ayer planned to preserve the animal with taxidermy as a mounted display and perhaps offer it to a museum. "It's definitely something I don't want to throw away," he said. "I think it will be an interesting mount and a tremendous conversation piece."

Canion also said she planned to preserve the head of her chupacabra as a mount, perhaps adding it to the other wildlife trophies hanging on her den wall from past hunting safaris in Africa. She jokingly told one reporter that she might have it mounted with "a stuffed chicken in its mouth."

Meanwhile, the debate continues. Is the chupacabra a reality or merely an urban legend? One Cuero resident is willing to have it either way: "It's like every good urban legend," he said, "maybe it's better to just think it is the chupacabra and just leave it at that." Though he claims to be a nonbeliever, Ayer voiced a similar attitude in a television interview: "I don't know what to call it; I'll just call it a chupacabra too."

Journalist Mike Cox points out that chupacabras "are third on the top three listing of mythical creatures, behind Big Foot and the Loch Ness monster." As such, they remain intriguing enough and popular enough in the minds of many to ensure a good market for T-shirts, bumper stickers, baseball hats, and other souvenir items. They have been the subjects of songs and movies, including *Scooby-Doo and the Monster of Mexico*. They have been investigated and analyzed by various television shows, such as *X-Files, Monster Quest,* and *Texas Snipe Hunt*. And each newly reported sighting gets picked up as a news story by the likes of CNN and the Associated Press.

The question that drives the curiosity is an age-old one that is summed up by Canion: "Is this an old boogie man thing that we are finding out is in fact reality? Could be."

CHAPTER 7

Legends of Enchanted Rock

Young John Coffee Hays—everybody called him Jack—talked to his pistols sometimes when he cleaned them. "I may not need you, but if I do, I will need you mighty bad." Right now he needed them.

He had set out alone that fall morning in 1841 to inspect Enchanted Rock, a great pink dome of granite rising out of the Llano valley. The rest of his party of twenty Texas Ranger surveyors remained in camp nearby on Crabapple Creek, but even closer was a band of Comanche. The warriors, protective of what they considered to be a holy mountain and angered by the intrusion of settlers in general, pursued and attacked. Hays rode his horse as far as he could up the rock face and then scrambled the rest of the way to the summit on foot.

He had his rifle and two Colt five-shooters and a fairly clear field of fire down the slope. But he was outnumbered about a hundred to one. Still, he was determined to sell his life at the "highest market price." Fortunately for him, the Comanche were reluctant to climb to the top of the round mountain lest they encounter the spirits they thought might roam there. Simply by deciding "to lay low and keep dark" and by occasionally brandishing his superior weapons, Hays was able to hold them off for an hour without even firing a shot. But in time the warriors rushed closer, and he began to fire, defending himself for another three hours. His men, meanwhile, had finally heard the crack of his rifle and came to his aid. The retreating Indians believed more than ever that Hays bore a charmed life.

What, then, were these tales of spirits that probably saved Hays's life as much as his five-shooters? There were several legends, actually, accumulated over the years as various groups of Native Americans inhabited the area. The Tonkawa, for example, told about a few brave warriors long ago who defended themselves for many years as the last of their tribe against hostile attacks from other Indians. In the end they were overcome and annihilated, but they remained on the rock as phantom warriors. The Tonkawa attributed to these spirits of the dead the "ghost fires" they saw flickering at the top and the mysterious creaking and groaning noises emanating from Enchanted Rock, for if the dead were not properly buried, their souls "were apt to hang around." This was especially true for the souls of men, whereas the souls of women, the Tonkawa believed, would "go directly to the home in the west singing as they went."

A conquistador captured by the Tonkawa managed to escape by hiding in the rock's caves and crevices and seeming to simply disappear. The Tonkawa then spoke of a "pale man swallowed by a rock and reborn as one of their own." They believed he had powers of enchantment, but the conquistador said it was the rock that was a weaver of spells. "When I was swallowed by the rock," he said, "I joined the many spirits who enchant this place."

By the early 1700s the Apache had moved in and created their own myths. For them, the Gan, or mountain spirits, lived forever in the mountain's caves. Sent by the Giver of Life to "teach the people a better way to live, govern, hunt, and cure illness," the Gan were benevolent and could be appealed to "for guidance and protection." Thus, for the Apache, Enchanted Rock truly was a sacred place.

The Comanche displaced the Apache by the end of the 1700s, and for them the pink granite dome was a destination for a vision quest. Second only to the sun, the Earth's natural monuments, such as Enchanted Rock, were objects of devotion, and the Comanche "would pay homage to the object of their veneration," go to sleep, and hope for a dream that would "reveal the counsel" they had prayed for. For them, too, Enchanted Rock was sacred.

The possibility that the Comanche engaged in human sacrifice is suggested in a legend probably passed on by early Spaniards and later collected as folklore by German settlers. A young Spanish soldier of fortune named Don Jesus Navarro, so the story goes, came from Monterrey, Mexico, to the San Jose y San Miguel de Aguayo Mission in San Antonio in 1750. There he met and fell in love with Rosa, a Christian convert and the daughter of an Indian chief named Tehuan.

When a band of Comanche attacked the mission, Navarro was knocked unconscious by a tomahawk blow to his head, and his beloved Rosa was kidnapped and carried away. Once he recovered his senses, Navarro mounted up, rode to Goliad to recruit help, and

Enchanted Rock is said to harbor ghosts in the Texas Hill Country.
DONALD RAY BOYD, PHOTOGRAPHER

set out to rescue his sweetheart. The men soon discovered a large Comanche campsite and surmised that the Indians were headed for Enchanted Rock, possibly to sacrifice Rosa to the spirit of the rock.

Sure enough, by the time the men reached Enchanted Rock, the Comanche had already tied Rosa to a stake, where they planned to burn her as a ritual offering. They were still piling pieces of wood at her feet as Navarro's men attacked from two sides. Navarro himself had only one mission: He rode through the startled warriors, cut the leather cords binding Rosa to the stake, and swung her up behind him on his horse. Then he guided his horse up onto the rock itself, defying, at least to the Comanche way of thinking, the spirit of the rock in the process. That was enough for the Comanche. They beat a hasty retreat, and Rosa was saved.

Other legends are likely tied to rumors that precious metals could be found in the area. Spanish explorers believed that Enchanted Rock "was one large chunk of silver or iron" or that gold or silver mines at least might be nearby. One persistent Indian legend suggested that "somewhere in the rock is a mine of pure silver." In the 1830s a group of young men supposedly traveled up the Colorado and Brazos Rivers searching for "a large rock of metal," said to be made of platinum. The Indians, they were told, would allow no white man to approach it, as they had considered it sacred for centuries and came once a year to worship it. Even if someone did reach the rock, that person would be unable to make so much as a dent on its surface with a hammer or chisel, and the sound of the striking "would bring out a ringing sound which could be heard for miles." If the search party was successful in finding the rock, there is no record of their having brought any pieces of platinum back with them.

The wife of a settler named James Webster was captured, along with her two young children, from a wagon train in 1838 by a band of Comanche. The captives were taken to Enchanted Rock. After two years they escaped from the Indians and made their way to San Antonio, where Mrs. Webster added to the lore of lost mines by telling of "gold and silver mines and brilliant stones the Indians possessed that looked like diamonds."

A smattering of legends of more uncertain origin remains in circulation as well. One describes an Indian princess who was so distraught by the slaughter of her people by enemy Indians that she threw herself off of Enchanted Rock. Her spirit is said to haunt the place. Then there are the footprints of an Indian chief doomed to walk the summit of the rock forever. His constant pacing has worn indentations in the stone. According to legend, he is being punished for taking his daughter to the rock's heights and sacrificing her during a time of famine to appease the devilish rock spirit. And, finally, one story suggests that screams sometimes audible in the night are those of a white woman kidnapped by Indians. Although she escaped, she continued to live on Enchanted Rock, but not in peace, apparently.

So, that fearsome chunk of granite—with its ghost warriors, spirit fires, mysterious voices, and blood sacrifices—was intimidating enough back in 1841 to hold the Comanche at bay and no doubt save Jack Hays's scalp. A plaque near the top of Enchanted Rock commemorates the battle. Hays went on to become quite a legend in his own right, exhibiting bravery that "bordered closely on rashness," according to J. W. Wilbarger, a contemporary of Hays's. Although small in stature, standing less than five feet eight inches tall, Hays "could shoot straighter, fight meaner, ride faster, cuss louder and endure hardships better than any man in his command." One of the Lipan Apache guides with whom he rode summed up Hays's fearlessness: "Me and Red Wing," Chief Flacco said, indicating another chief, "not afraid to go to hell together. Captain Jack heap brave—not afraid to go to hell by himself."

Today pilgrims still come to Enchanted Rock. As Ira Kennedy observes, "To this day Native Americans journey to this landmark for prayer and ceremony as do many people of other races and religions. Enchanted Rock inspires awe and reverence. There is a sense of being, of presence inherent to this unique monolith which is apparent even to this day. That will never change."

Tourists travel to see and climb the second-largest batholith (an underground rock formation uncovered by erosion) in the United States, covering a one-square-mile area, 640 acres. Only Georgia's Stone Mountain is larger. At its highest point Enchanted Rock's pink granite exfoliation dome is 1,825 feet above sea level, and it rises 425 feet aboveground. Technically, according to *The Handbook of Texas*, Enchanted Rock can also be called a granite pluton or a granite monadnock, and, to be geologically correct, it is "part of a rough, segmented ridge, which is in turn part of the surface expression of a large igneous batholith of middle Precambrian material intrusive into earlier metamorphic schists and gneiss." Loosely translated, that means it has been around for about a billion years and that what can be seen now has been exposed after long and extensive erosion.

Estimates are that humans have been visiting the site for more than 11,000 years. Although "the first well-documented explorations of the area did not begin until 1723 when the Spanish intensified their efforts to colonize Texas," according to the Texas Parks and Wildlife Department, Enchanted Rock was very likely seen and sometimes noted by European explorers as early as Alvar Nuñez Cabeza de Vaca, who traveled the area before 1536. Others in the sixteenth, seventeenth, and eighteenth centuries visited and described the unique landmark as well.

Captain Henry S. Brown gets credit for "discovering" Enchanted Rock in 1829. While on a mission to subdue some Waco and Tehuacana Indians who had been raiding among the settlers in Stephen F. Austin's new colony in Texas, Brown and thirty other men had two encounters. As they made their way to the headwaters of the Colorado River, the Texans skirmished with the Indians twice, the second time at a place called "the enchanted rock." In his report of the affair, Brown described the granite mountain and was thereafter frequently listed as its discoverer.

In all likelihood the "enchanted rock" name was already in general use by the time Brown saw and described the dome. It seems to be a logical derivation from "Spanish and Anglo-Texas interpretations of Indian legends and related folklore." As already noted, these tales "attribute magical and spiritual properties to the ancient landmark." The Indians, however, may have had a different designation. Ira Kennedy says there is no record of any specific Indian name given to the rock, but he offers his theory that Native Americans might have referred to the dome as "Hill of the Medicine Man."

It was the *New York Mirror,* probably, that helped make the Enchanted Rock name more or less official. In 1838 the newspaper published an account of a prospecting trip on the San Saba River that included mention of an "Enchanted" or "Holy Mountain" near the headwaters of Sandy Creek. The Comanche, in particular, the article said, regarded the mountain with "religious veneration" and frequently assembled there to perform pagan rites. Samuel C. Reid, in 1847, said that he was "unable to give . . . the cause why this place was so named, but nevertheless, the Indians had great awe, amounting almost to reverence for it, and would tell many legendary tales connected with it."

So now let's return to the legends and mysteries regarding Enchanted Rock. The mountain is said to whisper or creak or groan, especially at night. Some hear "devil voices" coming from its depths. Climbers say that at certain points their footsteps seem to "drum," as if the rock is hollow under their feet. Could there be a phantom warriors' tomb after all? At night "strange lights seem to crackle and burn here and there, a thing called spirit fires by the Indians," and, when it rains, the streams of water pouring down the sides of the mountain look like "molten silver." There have even been reports of a rainbow that ends its path on top of the rock and that might, as legend has it, lead a seeker not to a pot of gold but to a gold mine. Then there's that old chief, doomed to walk eternally, leaving his precise moccasin prints on the summit as he keeps his tragic vigil.

Compelling as the stories may be, inquiring minds have wanted scientific explanations for the ghostly phenomena. As early as the 1840s, German immigrant Baron Otfried Hans Freiherr von Meusebach—who simplified his name to John O. Meusebach when he got to Texas—was fascinated by the mysterious sounds people reported hearing on or from within Enchanted Rock. He hoped to learn the source of the sounds. Nowadays geologists explain that the creviced granite mass of Enchanted Rock is affected by "heated days and chilled nights" and will "shift with deep whispers." The contraction of the rock's outer surface as it cools results in the "weird creaking and groaning noises." As to that tomb-hollow sound underfoot, especially on the mountain's north slope, there is likely "an old granite layer splitting loose."

The nighttime lights are explained by scientists as reflections of moonlight off the mica or feldspar in the granite or off the water in the rain pools standing and sometimes rippled by the wind in indentations in the rock's surface. Even in the daytime the mica on the rock's surface glitters "like glass in the sunlight," but the glitter is even more dramatic "on clear nights after a rain." And when the rain is heavy enough to produce running streams down the sides of the huge boulder, those same reflections do indeed make the water seem to flow like molten silver. And what look eerily like the moccasin prints of someone striding back and forth near the top of the rock can be explained as being nothing more than potholes worn by centuries of water erosion.

First included in a land grant to Anavato Martinez and his wife, Maria Jesusa Trevino, in 1838, Enchanted Rock was owned by several other individuals before it was acquired by the Nature Conservancy of Texas in 1978 and then by the Texas Parks and Wildlife Department in 1984, when it was opened as Enchanted Rock State Natural Area. The entire park consists of 1,643.5 acres on Big Sandy Creek, north of Fredericksburg in Llano County. Already designated a National Natural Landmark in 1970, it was placed on the National Register of Historic Places in 1984. Every year more than 350,000 visitors are drawn to this "megalithic monument" to marvel at its geological uniqueness and, perhaps, to wonder at its legends.

CHAPTER 8

The Lure of the Marfa Lights

A good rancher always rounds up his strays, especially when winter is approaching. In the Chinati Mountains in west Texas, that sometimes means climbing about on terraced mesas and in rugged canyons.

Near the old mining town of Shafter, one man—one of those good ranchers—was in search of missing livestock one evening when he was caught high in the mountains by a sudden blizzard, a whistling blue norther. The wind and snow and abrupt drop in temperature were disturbing enough, but even worse was the darkness that enveloped him. Unable to see, he groped his way along rocky hillsides and stumbled along uncertain trails. His hands and feet grew numb with the cold, and he feared for his life—feared that he might freeze to death or that he might pitch over a precipice at any moment. He came to an unfamiliar outcropping of rock that he would have to go over or around. Cold, afraid, and lost, he began to feel his way around, inching along.

And then he saw the lights: several lights, flashing lights, welcome lights. Although he could never explain it, even to himself, he knew from the outset that the lights were friendly, and somehow they spoke to him. He could never explain that either, but he knew and understood their message: He was off-course, three miles south of Chinati Peak and headed in the wrong direction. Furthermore, he understood from the lights that he was dangerously near a precipice. He must follow the lights or he would die. He followed.

The lights led him to a small cave, shelter enough to save him from freezing. The largest light remained in the cave close enough beside him to provide light and even some warmth. He sensed somehow that these were spirits from long ago and, perhaps, far away, and they wanted to save him. He slept, and he survived.

The next morning the lights were gone, and so was the blizzard. He stepped out of the cave and found his way to the outcrop. Just beyond the outcrop, right where the lights had confronted him, was a sheer cliff. Had he gone just a few more steps the night before, he would have likely plunged to his death.

In time the rancher told this story to his daughter. She accepted it and passed it on. One of the people to whom she related the story was Ed Syers, journalist and author of *Ghost Stories of Texas*. He attributes the story to Mrs. W. T. Giddens of Sundown, Texas, explaining that "she grew up in the Chinatis near Shafter." Syers, whose book was published in 1981, doesn't say when he interviewed her or when her father had his experience with the lights, but he does suggest that this rancher is the one man who may have encountered the Marfa Lights up close and personal.

Of course, by now a great many people have seen the Marfa Lights, beginning at least as far back as the late 1800s, but most have seen them from afar. Currently, the designated viewing area provided by the Texas State Highway Department is a roadside parking turnout nine miles east of Marfa on the south side of US Highway 90, near an abandoned air base. The Chinati Mountains are about fifty miles to the south across Mitchell Flat, said to be "the playground of the Marfa Lights."

The question remains: Just what are the Marfa Lights? Are they manifestations of some otherworldly beings—perhaps ghosts or aliens? Can they be explained logically, scientifically? So far, the answer to the latter question is no, at least not to everyone's satisfaction.

Robert Reed Ellison, who gets credit for being the first to record a sighting of the mysterious phenomenon, experienced the lights in 1883. He thought they were Apache watchfires, cause for alarm among cowboys back in those days. Ellison, whose wife accompanied him by wagon, was driving cattle through Paisano Pass when he first saw a flickering light. But then the light seemed to split apart and begin to move about, disappear, and reappear. Other settlers told him they too had seen the lights, but when they investigated, they found no ashes or other indications of campsites.

Over the years other observers came up with other theories about the cause or the source of the lights. Some theories had to do with natural geological or atmospheric possibilities: moonlight reflecting off mica, phosphorescent minerals, luminous "swamp gas" or piezoelectric energy produced by small earthquakes, electrostatic illumination like Saint Elmo's fire, refracted starlight, ball

A viewing center marks the best spot to watch for the Marfa Lights.
MAX KANDLER, PHOTOGRAPHER

lightning or static electricity, atmospheric inversions or "bent" lights like mirages. Other theories were more imaginative or reflected concerns of the moment. Could the lights be unidentified flying objects from outer space or, perhaps, jackrabbits with glowworms on their tails? Observers during World War I worried that the lights might be some kind of waymarkers, guides for a possible enemy invasion. Today many people figure that the lights may be nothing more mysterious than vehicle headlights seen at a distance coming south through the mountains on US Highway 67 from Marfa to Presidio. Since there would have been no vehicle headlights in the 1880s, however, the debate goes on, as does the accumulation of folklore.

The most enduring legends are the ones about Alsate, the last of the Apache chiefs to live in the area in the mid-1800s. Some say the lights are his spirit itself, condemned to wander in the Chinatis because he offended a tribal god. But far more say that the lights are his watchfires as he seeks one who betrayed him and his people. The betrayal part of that legend is apparently true.

According to a story recorded by O. W. Williams, a surveyor in the Big Bend in the 1880s, it happened this way: The Mescalero Apache living in or near the Chisos Mountains, south of the Chinatis, were unwelcome in both Texas and Mexico and were pursued by authorities on both sides of the border. The Apache would evade the Texas Rangers by crossing the Rio Grande into Mexico and then cross back into Texas when the Mexican *rurales* got too close on their trail. Further provoking authorities were some renegade Mexicans who joined up with the Apache, and together "they made the Big Bend a hotbed for trouble."

Enter Lionecio Castillo, enlisted by the Mexicans to talk to Alsate and other Apache leaders and set them up for removal or extermination. His message was that the Mexican government wanted to make a treaty with the Apache and provide them with a reservation similar to ones established for Indians in the United States. On these reservations the Apache would be provided for, Castillo promised. He even had papers, fraudulent but impressive looking with gold seals and ribbons, to show Alsate and the others as "proof" of the government's intentions.

Even though he was wary, Alsate agreed that he and his band would come to San Carlos in Mexico to be "entertained with a grand fiesta." They would receive presents and provisions, Castillo said. Dubious as he was, Alsate nevertheless "gave the signal to enter the town, first placing sentinels on mountain tops nearby." And he was right to be suspicious, as several companies of Mexican soldiers were at that moment camped very near the city of San Carlos.

Once in town, the Indians did receive gifts. They partook of roasted beef and goat, and they drank the proffered *mescal*, a potent Mexican libation. By that evening, most of the men were drunk, and the sentinels, having seen no soldiers and feeling left out of the Mexicans' generosity, had abandoned their posts and joined the party. It was a simple matter then for the Mexican soldiers to move in during the night, surround the town, and capture and shackle all the Indians, "most of whom were in a drunken stupor." Before nightfall the Apache, manacled and strung out in long lines, were being marched toward Chihuahua and, ultimately, Mexico City. Many died on the way. Of the survivors, some died in prison; others "were distributed among the various families in southern Mexico as slaves." None returned to their homes in the Chisos Mountains—except maybe Alsate.

Williams doesn't say what Alsate's fate was at the hands of the Mexicans, but others provide two versions. One says he escaped and returned to the Chisos and Chinati Mountains searching for Castillo, his betrayer. The other is that Alsate died before a firing squad in San Carlos. The latter version has been confirmed by Alsate's grandson in an interview. In either case, rumors began to circulate that sheepherders and vaqueros in the Big Bend had seen the ghost of Alsate. Some said he was lighting campfires to summon his warriors back to help him find Castillo. Even his wife climbed up in the mountains to light her own fires, according to some.

Border residents grew fearful and were reluctant to go out at night. Mexican *rurales* searched the area. They found no ghost, but they did find a cave that showed signs of recent occupancy. Sure enough, that is where locals said the ghost appeared again and again, so it soon became known as Alsate's Cave. In time residents accepted the ghost and no longer worried about it—except for Lionecio Castillo. He was so unnerved by news of Alsate's ghost that he left the country. After a long time, Castillo returned. So did the ghost. Castillo disappeared again. Finally, according to Williams, the ghost was seen no more, "and the bravest and most curious decided to search the cave. There they found the remains of the great Chief Alsate near the ashes of a fire long dead."

Williams heard the story he recorded and later privately published from Natividad Lujan, a member of his surveying crew and a campfire storyteller. A complementary tale is one heard by James Cooper of Snyder and passed on by Elton Miles. It too has Castillo leaving the country in terror when Alsate's ghost was prowling around. But he didn't entirely escape. Making his way through the Chisos Mountains, Castillo took refuge in a large cave for the night. Recalling his own part in the betrayal of Alsate and the rest of the Apache, he looked out toward the moonlit peaks. That is when he saw on one of the ridges "the exact, terrifying features of Alsate's face." Even when Castillo turned away and faced the back of the cave, the shrieking winds took on the voice of Alsate "crying out for his soul." Castillo fled the cave.

Even today one may see Alsate's profile in stone. Those entering the Chisos from the north and driving south from Persimmon Gap can see it on the right. It seems carved into the west face of Casa Grande peak.

A less well-known story about Alsate's ghost as a possible source of the Marfa Lights has him falling in love with an Indian maiden. The young woman was loved by another, however, who vowed to kill his rival and followed Alsate and the maiden to their meeting place. There the angry would-be suitor accidentally killed the young woman instead of Alsate and carried her body away to hide it in the mountains. The lights, this legend says, are those of Alsate and the young woman searching for each other.

Over the years, curious and determined searchers have observed, chased, and photographed the lights. They have calculated, triangulated, and hypothesized in efforts to explain what the lights are and where they come from. And more legends have emerged.

At first, in the early 1900s, some of the more adventuresome cowboys went riding into the Chinati Mountains looking for the source of the lights. They found nothing. Then, during World War II, when Marfa Army Air Field was an active training base for military pilots, some of the trainees supposedly made it their mission to solve the mystery. They tried buzzing the lights from the air. They "bombed" them with sacks of flour as source markers. Surveyors and reporters followed up. Resulting reports stayed pretty much the same. Pursued lights would head toward Mexico or simply wink out. Morning investigations of the dropped flour bombs would reveal nothing more than white dust residue on the empty landscape.

Before long, stories began to circulate that suggested a more ominous than friendly cast to the lights. Investigating pilots were said to be lured to their deaths against the rocky cliffs of the

Chinati Mountains. Another rumor was that a civilian pilot once mistook the Marfa Lights as the landing lights of an airport and crashed while trying to land his plane. Wallace Chariton says none of these more modern legends are true, and "no reliable evidence has been uncovered to prove that the army has ever done anything concerning the lights."

He cites another example that turned out to be a calculated hoax. The tale often told is that a team of army experts drove a Jeep out onto the desert "determined to find out what the lights were or die trying." Sure enough, the men simply disappeared, and nothing was left but the burned-out shell of the Jeep. Later one man admitted that a bunch of soldiers did drive a Jeep—one they had stolen during a night of drinking—in search of the lights. They didn't find them, but the driver did hit a boulder, and the Jeep turned over. They set fire to the wrecked vehicle and made the lights the culprits in the cover story they concocted.

Other vehicular stories followed. A persistent one describes one light, sometimes said to be ten feet tall, chasing a car at speeds approaching 100 miles per hour. The light finally disappeared or quit the chase, and the driver discovered that the rear end of his car was scorched as if it had been in a fire. Chariton says, "It is a good story but there is absolutely no verification or evidence to prove it actually happened." The same could be said for other automobile-related tales, like the one about some out-of-state travelers on US Highway 90 who were confused by what they took to be reflectors on the side of the road. Their car was found gutted as if by fire, although the exterior was unharmed. Only coins, keys, and other nonflammable objects remained inside, but there was no sign of the travelers themselves. Yet another story in the same vein involves a boy and girl parked on the old airfield when the lights appeared. The frightened girl began to scream, so the boy started to drive away. The lights gave chase, gaining on the car. The young couple could feel the heat. When the tires blew out, the couple got out of the car and ran to safety. They came back the next day to discover the car melted and still smoking hot. In a more deadly version, the girl dies of shock during the ordeal, and only the boy goes back to the scene of the accident about a week later. He is never seen or heard from again.

It is likely that high school and college students with overactive imaginations account for a number of fairly recent stories. One is that some local high school students in a Jeep went out to see the lights and never returned. Those searching for them could find only their tire tracks, which ended abruptly in an arroyo. No other trace of the Jeep or the students was ever found. The Marfa Lights, so say the tellers of this tale, are the ghost headlights of the Jeep as the young people continue to signal in hopes of being rescued. Both Syers and Chariton mention that students at Sul Ross State University in nearby Alpine pass on stories about motorists being lured by the lights into head-on crashes on either US Highway 90 or 67. Again, local law enforcement agencies provide no verification that any such accidents have been caused by the mysterious lights, although there are recorded cases of motorists who have mistaken the lights for car lights and thought they might crash into another car. In each case, however, "the lights disappeared and no accident resulted."

Estimates are that more than seventy-five local folktales having to do with the Marfa Lights remain in circulation, and still people come to see and speculate, including those from the media. In 1980 a reporter, Stan Redding, and a photographer, Carlos Antonio Rios, from the *Houston Chronicle* were dispatched to "check out this Marfa light thing and see if there is anything to it." As the two men drove down a dirt road on the flats at Paisano Pass east of Marfa, the lights not only appeared but also seemed to "pose" while Rios took pictures. The lights were almost close enough to touch, the men said. Chariton quotes Redding's description: "They darted about the ground—red, white and blue orbs, baseball-sized. They would blend into one, then separate. One would zoom high into the air, then plummet down to disappear in the brush, only to pop up an instant later and spin away crazily. Unsupported and unattached, each illuminated the brush over which it hovered."

Others have offered similar descriptions since those first recorded sightings. There is always mention of movement, diagonally, horizontally, up and down, side to side, and of the lights disappearing and reappearing, blinking off and on or fading in and out. Generally one to three lights appear, and their colors can be white, green, blue, red, or some pastel shade like soft pink or pale yellow. Their size is likened to anything from baseballs to cantaloupes to basketballs. Hallie Stillwell, a rancher who lived in the Big Bend country almost all her life, said, "It looks like a big headlight. It just kind of flickers along the mountain. They might cover a section or two of land. They light up and run across the mountain, kind of like a grass fire."

In July 1989 camera crews and investigators from NBC's television show *Unsolved Mysteries* descended on Marfa. They conducted interviews with the locals and brought in scientists, technicians, and spotters. They marked with special lights the stretch of US Highway 67 that was visible from the viewing area to rule out the automobile headlight theory and then started filming. Appropriately, at one minute before midnight "an unknown light" appeared. Host Robert Stack said the light was "ghostly gold." The light faded from view and then returned as bright as before. The scientists agreed that the light was not man-made, but they could not agree on what caused it.

Then in May 1991 members of the Southwest Ghost Hunters Association filed their own investigation report. They went out on three separate occasions, they said, armed with "spectral data" on all kinds of automobile, city, and ranch lights. They took into account atmospheric conditions. In the end, they say, they "scientifically proved with a number of experiments" that the Marfa Lights they saw "were indeed only headlights coming from a distant road in the mountains on US Highway 67." Always open to new possibilities, however, they acknowledge that others have reported seeing mysterious and unexplained lights on the horizon to the left of where the headlights appeared. They "were not lucky enough to witness these," they say, and allow that they might go out again to repeat their experiment to "see if we get the same results." This group also calls into question the report of Robert Ellison, the cowboy who supposedly first saw the Marfa Lights in 1883. That information is secondhand, according to the ghost hunters, since Ellison was interviewed in 1937 and is quoted in someone else's book. In his own memoirs Ellison does not mention the lights, but he did apparently tell his family about having seen them. His daughter, Mrs. Lee Plumbley, has repeated the story of his encounter as being true. As to the headlights, Chariton, who spends much of his time debunking legends, points out that if automobile lights are the answer, they would have to move always from left to right as cars come toward Marfa from Presidio. But the lights sometimes move from right to left, meaning that "if cars are the cause, someone is backing up at a high rate of speed, at night, on a dangerous mountain highway."

Whatever they are, the Marfa Lights are predictable, showing up on average three hundred nights a year. They are a major tourist attraction, and Marfa celebrates that fact with the Marfa Lights Festival on Labor Day weekend each year. Interestingly enough, however, a recent newspaper article about "The Lure of Marfa" mentioned the arts, music, and culinary scene in the small city but included not one word about the Marfa Lights. Still, the greatest lures undoubtedly are those lights and the mystery that surrounds them. Perhaps Chariton sums it up best: "For those of us who appreciate a good mystery and an even better legend, the prospect that the best little Texas mystery of all time will never be solved is not particularly unsettling."

CHAPTER 9

The Haunting of Jefferson

It was almost eight o'clock on a Monday night in Jefferson, Texas, when Mitchel and Tami Whitington realized they had forgotten to grab the container of dinner leftovers out of their car and bring it to their room. Mitchel hurried as he went to get it because a television program they wanted to watch was about to start.

They were staying in the Jay Gould Room on the second floor of the east wing of the historic Excelsior House in Jefferson. Mitchel walked quickly down the stairs, crossed the foyer, and entered a hallway. As he did, he smelled the overwhelming scent of perfume. Whew, he thought, some woman must have doused herself pretty heavily right here on this spot. It was probably another guest in the hotel, he reasoned, even though he and Tami hadn't seen anyone but the desk clerk since they had arrived.

On his way back from the car, he stopped to talk to the desk clerk in the lobby before he opened the door back into the hallway. The strong perfume smell was still there, not dissipated in the least, although it seemed to Mitchel that it might have moved a little nearer the lobby.

He told Tami about the experience, and during the next commercial break in their TV program, they both went to check out the phenomenon. This time it was Tami who found herself in the middle of the perfume cloud at the bottom of the staircase. She smelled both perfume and makeup, she said, but still no one was in sight. Mitchel realized that the smell had moved from the hallway to the staircase and had lost none of its potency.

They returned to their room but explored again during the next commercial break, about fifteen minutes later. The foyer at the bottom of the stairs was now odor free, as was the lobby end of the hallway, but apparently the perfumed person, or spirit, had simply moved again, and Tami encountered the smell at the other end of the hallway where the guest rooms were. It was as strong as ever.

Another fifteen minutes later, they conducted another search. The perfume cloud had moved to the other end of the hallway again, closer to the lobby than before, and this time Mitchel and Tami sensed movement even as they stood near the smell. It was then that they decided to go out by the fountain in the courtyard to enjoy the moonlit evening and get away from the unexplained for a while. They were outside for thirty or forty-five minutes.

Once back inside the hotel, however, they couldn't resist exploring the hallway one more time, and, sure enough, the perfume cloud had continued moving back down toward the foyer again. Tami went to the lobby to ask the clerk if she was wearing perfume. Yes, she was. Maybe that's the explanation, Tami thought, until the clerk said she hadn't been near the hallway for hours. When Tami explained what she and Mitchel had experienced, the desk clerk said, "This isn't the first time something like this has been reported."

Could it be another guest?

"Oh, no," the desk clerk said, "you're the only ones registered."

So, is it true that Jefferson is the most haunted city in Texas, as some claim? And just how many ghosts might be moving around in the Excelsior House, said to be the most haunted hotel in the city? It's hard to say, but one visitor posted a review after a stay at the hotel in June 2003 giving it a five-star rating straight across with only one minor complaint: "the ghosts, but they aren't that scary."

Another guest, genealogist Judy Sander Cockrell, was a little more explicit about what she called the "ghostly ambiance":

> *During the entire stay at the Excelsior, I felt as if I were on a boat. It seems as though the entire building is a tad leaning toward the back. It made me rather dizzy at first, until I got used to it. Not an easy thing to describe, obviously, but trust me on this one. Rockers have been known to suddenly rock, clawfoot bathtubs suddenly stop running water, only to have the sink begin to flow. Knocking noises in the walls, and footsteps through the halls are just a few of the true stories I read about in the journal that I found in my room.*

When questioned in 2009 about the existence of any such journal, by the way, desk clerk Mary Fredrickson said she knew nothing about it. She had heard about the perfumed spirit, however.

Retired ABC newsman Lyndon (Dave) Adams and his wife spent a night in the Gould Room at the Excelsior in September

1995. He too smelled perfume and said he saw "the figure of a woman dressed all in black, with a black veil" standing beside the bed as he crossed the room from the bathroom. Then she simply vanished. While in the bathroom he had noticed that the bathroom door was swinging open, so he shut it, making sure it latched. Then when he tried to open the door and return to bed, the knob wouldn't turn. It was as if "something or someone was apparently gripping the knob on the other side, tightly." Finally, the pressure let up, and he could open the door.

Adams managed to get back to sleep, but he awoke several more times, once to the odor of cigar smoke and the sound of someone turning newspaper pages, once because of knocking and fingernail-dragging sounds on the headboard, and once to noises in the bathroom, even the sound of a flushing toilet. His wife remembered only the sound of knocking. At least the Adamses stayed the night through.

Not so in the case of Steven Spielberg, the well-known director of films such as *E.T., Close Encounters of the Third Kind,* and *Poltergeist.* A couple of authors, Frank X. Tolbert and Kent Biffle, cite a *Dallas Morning News* article quoting Spielberg as saying he spent a night at the Excelsior in the early 1970s while he was in Texas filming *Sugarland Express.* "I swear my room was haunted," he said. "I made everybody wake up, pack up, and get back in the cars at about two o'clock in the morning. We had to drive twenty miles to the nearest Holiday Inn and everybody was hot at me." Spielberg added that he was "not normally superstitious." Desk clerk Fredrickson confirmed that story.

Tolbert also reported hearing from a woman who stayed in the Hayes Presidential Room at the Excelsior back in 1979. The ghost in her room was a bit more playful, it would seem, as she reported that it "kept pulling the covers off the high four-poster bed," and another woman in the adjoining Grant Presidential Room perceived an "unseen presence breathing heavily" in the bathroom.

As the room designations suggest, the Excelsior House has played host to a number of famous people since it opened in the 1850s. The two presidents for whom rooms are named, Rutherford B. Hayes and Ulysses S. Grant, stayed there, as did the "robber baron" railroad magnate Jay Gould, John Jacob Astor, W. H. Vanderbilt, Oscar Wilde, Lyndon and Lady Bird Johnson, and George W. and Laura Bush, to name a few. Legend has it that Gould left without paying his bill in January 1882 and wrote at the bottom of the page he signed in the hotel register, "The end of Jefferson!" The register is on display in the Excelsior lobby as proof of his prediction. The only indication that he may have skipped out on his bill is the "X" beside his name rather than a dollar amount and a check mark, as is the case with other guests listed on the same date. Gould was angry at the citizens of Jefferson, so the story goes, either because the town wouldn't grant him land for his railroad line or because they wouldn't pay him a bonus to establish machine shops for his railroad there. Current Jefferson residents can recite Gould's "curse," uttered by him during his visit and reported in local newspapers at the time: "May bats roost in your belfries, and may grass grow in your streets, oh, you decadent port."

As a fitting postscript to the story, the same garden club that later bought and restored the Excelsior House found, bought, and restored Gould's personal Pullman Company railcar "Atalanta," built in 1888, and installed it across the street from the hotel in 1954. It is now a tourist attraction.

Another of the Excelsior's rooms is named for a locally famous woman buried in Jefferson's Oakwood Cemetery. The fact that the Diamond Bessie Suite is designated as the bridal suite seems a little ironic since Diamond Bessie was allegedly a prostitute who was murdered by her lover, although the case was never officially solved. Locals still remember tales about the sensational murder trial that resulted from the crime and stage a reenactment of it every year as part of the Jefferson Historic Pilgrimage.

In brief, the story goes like this: A woman calling herself Bessie Moore arrived in Jefferson in the 1870s with her consort, Abraham Rothschild. They registered, not at the Excelsior but at the Brooks House, as A. Monroe and wife. On the Sunday morning after they arrived, Rothschild bought picnic lunches, and the couple disappeared into the fog as they crossed a footbridge over Big Cypress Creek. Only Rothschild returned, and he subsequently left town alone.

Snow and bad weather hampered the search for the missing woman, but a week or so later her body was found near a tree alongside the remains of a picnic lunch. She died from a gunshot wound to the head, the coroner ruled. Concerned citizens in Jefferson took up a collection and buried her in the Oakwood Cemetery.

In time, Rothschild was arrested, tried, and convicted, but, on appeal, a judge declared a mistrial because one of the jurors had admitted he had a prior opinion in the case. During a second trial the defense produced a witness who said she had seen Bessie in the company of another man. True or not, it was enough to plant a seed of doubt in the minds of the jurors, and this time Rothschild was found not guilty. From beginning to end, the legal battle took two and a half years.

Not until 1930 did Bessie, whose real name was Annie Stone, have a headstone, and in the 1960s the Jessie Allen Wise Garden Club had an iron fence built around her grave.

In 1961 that same garden club bought the Excelsior House, did major restorations, furnished it with fine period antiques, and kept it open throughout the whole process. In fact, the Excelsior is the oldest continuously operated hotel in Texas. The garden club continues to manage the hotel, and the representatives don't particularly want to talk about any resident ghosts.

The Excelsior House Hotel is only one of the buildings said to house ghosts in Jefferson.
PAUL PORTER, PHOTOGRAPHER

The Jefferson Hotel right across the street, however, has willingly listed several stories of ghostly experiences at the hotel. A number of them seem to correspond to those described at the Excelsior: knocks on walls and headboards, the smell of cigar smoke, faucets opening of their own accord, doors pulling back when shut, and so forth. Others are particular to the Jefferson. A former desk clerk named Michael claims to have been scared into the street one night as he was locking up. He was closing the last door in a long, dark hallway, he said, when all the doors started opening and closing at once and lights turned on and off. He heard footsteps and the sound of someone dragging furniture. At that point, he decided to stand outside to wait for his ride home that night.

A young guest in room 5 repeatedly saw "a man in a long coat and high boots," and a ninety-year-old guest said he saw a "petite blonde woman floating down the stairs smiling at him." She disappeared before she reached the bottom step. That could be the same thin, long-haired blonde sighted in or near room 12. One woman said her husband saw shadows passing across the lighted crack under the door in room 12—from the inside. Yet they were the only guests in the hotel that night. Once her husband had gone to bed, he claimed he felt a hand moving up and down his leg, as if in a caress. A petite woman, perhaps the same blonde, has also appeared in room 19, where a man said this apparition "chilled [his] wife's arm with a touch of her hand."

Room 19 is also where a man and his wife saw writing on the bathroom mirror one morning. Having drawn a hot bath, the wife watched the mirror fog up from the steam. Slowly, she said, the word *Help* appeared in the middle of the mirror. She called her husband in to see just as the word *Judy* faded in above the first word. Then, at the bottom, came the letters *EDRUM*, filling the width of the mirror. Finally, a small *r* seemed fingered in above the *E*. *Murder*, spelled backward, they deciphered. According to legend, a young prostitute was murdered in that room, although there is no documented evidence to support the claim. She was supposedly attacked and left to die in the bathtub.

Another story tells of an 1890s bride-to-be who hanged herself when her groom sent word that he was not coming to marry her. The bed in that room was later moved to another room, and some say her ghost moved with it.

Then there's The Grove, now a private residence but open for scheduled tours. In this town of ghostly superlatives, it lays claim to being "the most haunted site in Texas" and is listed as "one of the top twelve historic haunted houses in America" by the television show *This Old House*. Currently owned by Mitchel and Tami Whitington, the same couple who tracked the perfumed spirit in the Excelsior House, The Grove was built in 1861 by Frank and Minerva Stilley.

The first recorded hint of a haunting came in 1882 when a man named T. C. Burks purchased the home and moved in with his family. They left within six months' time, saying only, "We can't live here." Charles and Daphnie Young and their family moved into the house in 1885 and had more staying power. Their older daughter, Louise, lived at The Grove her entire life, ninety-six years. Early on, Louise told her friends about "haints" at the house, apparently with some amusement. Later the ghost stories turned darker, and she was said to be terrified of the spirits that she saw walking around in her mother's garden. When she would turn on the porch light, the figures would disappear, so she ultimately had a security light installed in the garden. Still she was worried about someone getting inside the house and reportedly "called the police on a regular basis complaining about prowlers." Toward the end of her life, "she moved into just a few rooms of the house, letting the rest of the place start to deteriorate."

Coincidentally, a couple named Grove bought The Grove (probably named for a stand of pecan trees surrounding it) in 1983. They reported hearing "unexplained voices, disembodied footsteps," and "sounds of objects being moved by unseen hands." They also saw apparitions such as the one Mrs. Grove described after she fell asleep in her bedroom with her Bible nearby. She said she woke up to see "a black swirling mass engulfing the bedroom."

In 1990 Patrick Hopkins bought The Grove and, with his sister Mary, turned it into a restaurant. During the twelve years he owned it, Patrick reported a number of mysterious events: mirrors falling off the walls; loud wails coming from upstairs; unexplained moisture appearing in spots; and his constant feeling of being watched. Patrick also noted the presence of a ghostly woman, dressed in white. In a letter to author Docia Schultz Williams, he recalled the exact date and time—Friday, July 26, 1991, at 4:45 p.m.—that he first saw "a woman in a long white dress with puffed sleeves." The restaurant was to open at 5:00 p.m., and he had stopped in a hallway to dust an old trunk that had belonged to Louise Young. He heard footsteps coming from the kitchen and thought they were Mary's. Instead, this white-clad spectral stranger passed him and disappeared into the ladies' powder room, which had once been a bedroom. When he checked the powder room, no one was there.

Two years later, in May 1993, The Grove featured a dinner theater production of a murder mystery called *Angel Street*. The actors were in period costumes. During a dress rehearsal a lighting technician named Jennifer was on the front porch with some equipment as she watched the action inside through a window. Sensing someone staring at her, she turned to the right. There was the lady in white. As the lady started walking along the east side of the house, Jennifer followed, but the lady had disappeared. Meanwhile, the lead actress, Molly Gold, was coming down the stairs inside the house. As she reached the bottom step, she saw someone "in costume" standing in a corner. Thinking it was a cast member, Molly spoke, and the lady vanished.

During a Christmas Candlelight Tour seven months later, a Dallas-area couple took a picture of the Christmas lights on the neighboring house just east of The Grove. In the foreground of one photograph is "a lady in a high-collared, puff-sleeved white dress" surrounded by a "smoke ring." Following that incident, a neighbor living a block behind The Grove said she and her sister were standing on their porch about nine o'clock one night when they saw a "glowing white figure" across the street.

Current owner Mitchel Whitington thinks he knows who the most persistent ghost is. He is convinced that Minerva Stilley, the original owner of the house, is the "lady in white who haunts the east side of the house, steps through a wall, and strolls the interior." She is still walking through the house and grounds as they once were, he explains. "The wall she steps through to enter the house was an addition made in 1870." Most of the time during which Minerva lived there, the house had a back porch and an entrance where the wall is now. Old habits are hard to break.

Capitalizing on its reputation for being haunted, Jefferson advertises the Historic Jefferson Ghost Walk, an hour-and-a-half trek through the streets of town, starting on a downtown corner just after sunset. Standing outside the Excelsior House during the tour in 2009, guide Jodi Breck recalled working there as a night clerk. She said one evening when there were no registered guests, she was the only one in the hotel. After the front doors were locked at nine o'clock, she retired to a room on the first floor that is just below the Hayes Presidential Room. Breck said she heard what sounded like furniture being moved upstairs. She went to investigate and found the Hayes Room empty. But then she heard voices, seeming to come from across the hall or in the attic. One was a woman's voice with a German accent, and she knew that one of the earlier owners of the hotel was a German woman. Perhaps it is that experience that has prompted Breck to put the Excelsior very high on her list of Jefferson's most haunted places. Participants on her tour are encouraged to take pictures and use recorders on the chance that they might capture visual or aural evidence of "lingering spirits." Some say they have.

CHAPTER 10

Spirits in San Antonio

El Presidente sent the orders: Blow up the Alamo. Burn it down. Tear it down. Destroy it. Even in captivity, defeated at San Jacinto, General Antonio López de Santa Anna was in command of his forces, still the Napoleon of the West.

It fell to General Juan Jose Andrade to carry out Santa Anna's orders before he and the Mexican forces still in San Antonio moved out of the city. He called on a colonel named Sanchez to take a detail and demolish what was left of the old mission-turned-fortress. Only six weeks after the bloody battle the Mexican army waged and won in an effort to quell the Texas revolution, the Alamo's scars were already showing fresh and deep. Ashes and fresh-turned dirt were evidence of bodies burned and buried. Still Santa Anna wanted this symbol of Texans' resistance removed from the landscape—absolute victory, with no quarter given.

The orders were simple enough, Colonel Sanchez thought, as he and his contingent of soldiers approached the Alamo. But they never managed to detonate their charges in the chapel or torch the long barracks.

"*Diablos*," the men began to murmur as they saw six forms take shape and emerge from the front of the chapel. "*Diablos*," the men said louder as the phantoms moved into formation in a semi-circle. "*Diablos!*" the men shouted when the ghostly sentries raised flaming swords and defied the soldiers to come any closer. "*Diablos! Diablos! Diablos!*" the men continued to cry in a chorus as they turned and ran back to camp, refusing to return to the Alamo, no matter what the orders.

When Colonel Sanchez reported his failed mission to General Andrade, the general angrily scoffed at the idea that any devilish spirits might be guarding the Alamo and decided to take care of the demolition himself. He recruited a fresh contingent of men. They moved out toward the Alamo and were met by the same six figures, this time advancing with balls of fire in their hands and shouting, "Do not touch the walls of the Alamo!" Needing no further warning, Andrade's men fled in terror as the specters hurled the balls of fire in their direction. And Andrade sent no more destruction details but retreated as quickly as possible, leaving Santa Anna's orders unfulfilled.

The final battle for the Alamo went to the Texans after all.

That is one of the earliest tales, but certainly not the only ghostly legend associated with the Alamo. As several writers have observed, in a place where so many died so violently—estimates are that upwards of 400 to 600 Mexicans and at least 189 Texans were killed in the March 6, 1836, battle—it's no wonder that restless spirits still wander. The bodies of the vanquished Texans were denied Christian burial, stacked "like cordwood," and burned; slain Mexican soldiers were buried in shallow graves or thrown into the river. Still, one could question just who, exactly, these ghostly protectors of the Alamo might have been.

The popular notion is that the spirits of some of the dead defenders of the Alamo rallied to the defense once more. Author Docia Schultz Williams suggests that the spirits could have come from either side, "Mexican, Texian, or both." She says that "one thing was certain: They did not want the chapel destroyed, not after they had fought so hard and died so valiantly in the great battle." Another theory is that ghosts of Franciscan monks who occupied the Mission San Antonio de Valero prior to its being used as a fort might have come forth to protect the sanctity of the shrine.

Although the six ghostly figures are most often cited as the ones who frightened away the Mexican soldiers, two other manifestations are mentioned occasionally as well. The more common of those two describes one giant figure rising from the flames of a still-smoldering funeral pyre or standing atop the mission brandishing a ball or, sometimes, two balls of fire. Kathy Weiser points out that the cenotaph monument to the Alamo defenders, erected in 1939 and standing in front of the Alamo, depicts what could be this single spirit upon its face. "Legend has it," she says, "that when the ethereal energy was released from the flames where the Alamo defenders' bodies were burned, the spirit utilized the energy to make itself visible to frighten away the would-be destructionists." A third version is recorded by Jo-Anne Christensen. She says that "soldiers were frightened away from their demolition task by ghostly hands protruding from the walls and brandishing lit torches. As the men cowered in fear, a hollow, spectral voice intoned, 'Depart! Touch not these walls! He who desecrates these walls shall meet a horrible fate!'"

Reports of paranormal sightings have continued in the years following the fall of the Alamo. At least one ghostly sentry stayed on duty, apparently, according to an 1894 article in the *San Antonio Express-News*. At that time, the Alamo complex was being used as a police department, and night-duty officers said they heard the "same measured tread" of someone crossing the south side of the roof, always from east to west and always on rainy or drizzly nights. Because rainy weather accompanied the 1836 siege at the Alamo, the lone sentry was presumed to be from that period.

The same newspaper article described the visit of Leon Mareschal and his daughter, Mary, age fourteen, who visited the police headquarters one night with an interesting claim. Mary, her father said, was a medium and could communicate with the ghosts of the Alamo. Amused but skeptical, the officer in charge, Captain Jacob Coy, invited the pair to have a seat and see what happened. Mareschal hypnotized Mary, who said in a faint voice that she saw men, "spirits of the Alamo." She said that they were looking for $540,000 in $20 gold pieces buried in the walls. Coy was curious enough to ask for more specifics about the gold's whereabouts. Mary pointed vaguely to a corner of the Alamo before she came out of her trance, and then she and her father disappeared into the night. Another buried-treasure legend claims that the Alamo defenders, before the impending battle, placed their valuables in one of the mission bells and buried it. To date no buried gold or other valuables have been found.

According to some observers, the ghosts of a couple of celebrities show up from time to time. Park rangers have reported seeing a somewhat transparent figure wearing buckskin clothing and a coonskin cap standing at attention at various locations around the Alamo. He is holding a flintlock rifle. The assumption is that this is the spirit of none other than David Crockett, the well-known hunter and politician from Tennessee who fought and died at the Alamo. Of more recent vintage is the ghost of the Duke himself, John Wayne. Wayne produced and directed the 1960 film *The Alamo* and starred as David Crockett. Although he had his movie set constructed in Bracketville, Wayne and his set designers did extensive research at the Alamo in San Antonio. The result was an impressive three-quarter-scale replica of the mission that required two years to construct. The historical accuracy of the script, however, is another matter. Both J. Frank Dobie and Lon Tinkle, historical advisers for the film, asked that their names be removed from the credits. Nevertheless, Wayne had what bordered on an obsession about the movie. His daughter Aissa said, "I think making *The Alamo* became my father's own form of combat. More than an obsession, it was the most intensely personal project in his career." Perhaps that is why visitors reported seeing his spirit revisiting the Alamo beginning shortly after his death in 1979. He is described as apparently talking with some of the fallen defenders.

Even though the Alamo gift shop wasn't built until the 1930s, a persistent ghost presumed to be from the nineteenth century shows up there every year. A small blond boy, visible only from the waist up, peers down from a high interior window in the shop. He is most often seen in February, the anniversary of the time period when soldiers and their families began to arrive in the Alamo in 1836. According to legend, the boy, said to be between ten and twelve years old, was one of the children evacuated before the battle began while his father, perhaps, or brother or uncle remained to fight. Now the boy returns, looking for his relative. Not only is the sad face of the young boy enough to startle onlookers, but his mysterious appearance is all the more amazing because there is no way to climb up to the window and no ledge to stand on to peer through it.

Only the chapel and the long barracks remain of the original Alamo complex, for guardian sentries were not so successful in their efforts to preserve and protect in 1871 when the City of San Antonio decided to demolish two rooms on either side of the south wall's main gate. Guests at the Menger Hotel, across the street from the Alamo, reportedly watched as ghostly forms appeared and marched along the walls of the condemned rooms. The city tore them down anyway.

The Menger itself has ghosts, some of them possibly left over from the time of the Alamo battle. One of those is a ghost that was sighted by a hotel guest in his room and described in Docia Schultz Williams's book *The History and Mystery of the Menger Hotel*. It was the figure of a man wearing "a tan buckskin shirt, gray trousers, and an old, floppy brimmed brown felt hat." The ghostly intruder seemed to be in conversation with someone else, "someone the guest could not see." All the guest could make out was a question: "Are you going to stay, or are you going to go?" And the apparition muttered something about "Walker" before it disappeared. Although two psychics theorized that the spirit might have dated

The Alamo reportedly still has its share of spirits in San Antonio.
Donna Ingham, photographer

back to the beginning of the Civil War, Williams thinks it is just as likely that it might have been a spirit from 1836 debating with another spirit about whether to stay and defend the Alamo or to leave while it was still possible. She reminds her readers that the Menger "was built on land that belonged to the Mission San Antonio de Valero, where the famous Alamo chapel is located." She also points out that one of the defenders of the Alamo was a man named Jacob Walker from Tennessee, who might well have been dressed in buckskin, "common attire in those days."

In 2003, two hotel employees heard "heavy footsteps and kicking" as they walked toward the catering office. When they entered the room, however, they saw only a pair of military boots sitting near the door. Whether the boots might have belonged to the Walker ghost the employees couldn't say, and there have been at least two other military personages whose spirits are said to haunt the hotel. One might be that of Robert E. Lee, who did stay at the Menger shortly after it opened in 1859. A ghostly figure resembling the white-bearded Lee has been spotted by hotel staff members in the patio area and in one of the corridors leading to a new wing. The specter is dressed in Confederate gray, wearing high-top boots and a broad-brimmed campaign hat. He has a sword and scabbard hanging from his belt. The problem with this picture is that Lee would have been wearing a Union blue uniform in 1859, two years before the start of the Civil War. Williams argues that the spirit is more likely that of one of Lee's most trusted Confederate officers, General Kirby Smith, who was a guest at the hotel right after the war and who bore "a remarkable resemblance to Lee."

Another ghostly man in uniform seems to prefer hanging out in the Menger Bar, now called the Roosevelt Bar. That would be, appropriately enough, the spirit of Theodore (Teddy) Roosevelt, the twenty-sixth president of the United States. He first visited San Antonio and stayed at the Menger well before he became president, however. In the spring of 1892, he arrived to hunt javelina. By then a new bar had replaced the original, rather ordinary saloon, and this one had all the elegance and style of the pub at the English House of Lords, after which it was patterned. Roosevelt returned in the spring of 1898, this time to recruit men to fight in the Span-ish-American War. The unit he raised would become known as the Rough Riders, and many of its members were recruited there in the bar and trained at Fort Sam Houston in San Antonio. In

1905 Roosevelt made one final visit to the hotel, as president, for a reunion of the Rough Riders.

Perhaps Teddy has made subsequent visits as well, albeit not in his corporeal form. One custodian at the Menger, as he was doing some after-hours cleaning, reported seeing a man dressed in an old-fashioned military uniform sitting at the end of the bar in the early morning hours. A follow-up search by the night manager and a hotel security guard revealed nothing. Could it have been Teddy? At least one hotel manager and other employees and guests remain convinced that Roosevelt's ghost has come repeatedly to have a drink at the dark little bar off the main lobby. And Teddy also gets credit for ringing the front desk bell, even after it was disconnected, demanding the usual prompt service he had become accustomed to at the Menger. During some fairly recent remodeling, the bell was removed entirely.

Meanwhile, the spirit of Captain Richard King, of King Ranch fame, prefers to make itself at home in the suite King occupied as a frequent resident at the Menger. The King Suite, as it is now called, was—and still is—furnished with period furniture, including a big four-poster bed. King died in that bed in April 1885, at age sixty, and his funeral service was conducted in the Menger's front parlor. Since then, a number of hotel guests and employees claim to have seen his ghost entering the suite, not by the door currently in use but through the wall where the door used to be.

No sampler of Menger ghosts would be complete without mention of the most often sighted one of all, Sallie White. She was a biracial chambermaid who worked at the hotel in 1876. A good worker and well liked, she seemed to enjoy her time there and might have even felt safe there. For she was in a stormy relationship with her common-law husband, Henry Wheeler, and they often had loud and sometimes public quarrels. In late March 1876 Wheeler confronted her at the hotel and threatened her. She didn't go home after work. Instead, she spent the night at the courthouse waiting until morning to return to her house. Wheeler was waiting with a gun. She ran, and he pursued, finally overtaking her in the street. He fired, hitting her first in the abdomen and then in the back. Carried to her home, she survived for only two days. Wheeler was arrested but then subsequently released. He left San Antonio and was never traced or brought to justice. According to a ledger entry, the Menger Hotel paid $25 for Sallie's coffin and $7 for her grave site.

Now Sallie has become the Menger's "most famous spiritual ghost." As if continuing her duties there, she is most often seen at night walking the halls of the old Victorian wing dressed in her maid's uniform: a distinctive long gray skirt and a bandanna tied around her forehead. Sometimes observers mention a long string of beads around her neck and an apron. She is frequently described as carrying an armload of clean towels.

The Menger has claimed to be a "vault for vanquished spirits, with at least 32 different apparitions competing for sightings." Ernesto Malacara, director of public relations and a longtime employee, puts the number at forty-three. As if in explanation, the hotel website points out that the Menger was "built just steps from the battle of the Alamo and only 23 years after its bloody conclusion"; therefore, it's understandable that "the land lends itself to folklore."

And then there's the Gunter, another downtown hotel in San Antonio and the site of an unsolved mystery. Some facts of the case are well enough known. On February 2, 1965, a young man, blond and probably in his late thirties, checked into the Gunter Hotel. He signed in as Albert Knox and was given the key to room 636. During the next several days, he was seen in the company of a tall, blonde, sophisticated-looking woman.

On the afternoon of February 8, a maid saw the DO NOT DISTURB sign on the doorknob of room 636 but thought it was left there by mistake. She opened the door with her passkey. When she entered the room, she saw the man called Knox standing beside the blood-soaked bed and screamed. Knox lifted his index finger to his lips as if to silence her, gathered up a bloody bundle, and ran past her out the door.

Police detectives arrived to begin their investigation and discovered blood everywhere: on the bed, the carpets, the walls. They found small pieces of flesh in the bathroom and a .22-caliber slug in the bedroom wall. The shell of a fired .22-caliber bullet lay on the bed.

Within days, the police determined that the man they now suspected of murder was named Walter Emerick. They also learned that he had recently purchased a heavy-duty meat grinder at a San Antonio department store. The grisly possibilities were that Emerick had killed his companion, dissected and ground her body, and tried to dispose of it down the commode. What was left of the victim he carried out in the bloody bundle.

Tracking Emerick to the St. Anthony Hotel, a few blocks from the Gunter, detectives approached his door. A shot rang out, and by the time police forced their way into the room, Emerick was taking his last breath. The woman's body was never found. Because police discovered traces of a green dye used to color cement on Emerick's shoes, one theory is that the suspected killer buried parts of his victim in the wet cement of some downtown construction projects.

No woman matching the blonde's description has ever been reported missing, and the case is still open. Solved or not, the alleged murder is not likely to be forgotten, in part because of some unusual "happenings" reported from time to time in the vicinity of room 636 at the Gunter. Staff members and guests have attested to seeing a woman with her arms outstretched and of hearing sounds of hammering in sixth-floor rooms that are unoccupied.

Certainly it is evident that San Antonio—claimed by some to be "the most haunted city in the state of Texas"—has enough ghosts to warrant at least three advertised ghost hunt tours in the city. All three meet near the Alamo, said to be "the most haunted location in San Antonio." That makes it a very good place to begin and end.

CHAPTER 11

Children of the Tracks

Even the skeptics will try it: approaching a railroad crossing in south San Antonio, switching off the car engine, shifting into neutral, and waiting. But not for long. Sure enough, within seconds the car is moving from a dead stop, seemingly uphill, up to and then over the railroad tracks, finally coming to a stop around a curve in the road. If the skeptics have had the foresight to dust their trunk lids or bumpers with baby powder, or even if they sprinkle the powder on after the ride, oftentimes handprints or fingerprints appear as if providing evidence that unseen spirits have pushed the vehicle. And, of course, there's a story—several stories, actually—to go along with the experience.

Back in the 1930s, some say, a school bus stalled on those same tracks. Likely the children on the bus were doing what children do: making noise. So no one heard or saw that a freight train was bearing down on them. Nevertheless, the bus driver was trying frantically to restart the bus, and certainly the train engineer was trying frantically to stop the train. Neither succeeded, and the train hit the bus broadside, splitting it in two and carrying the back half some distance down the tracks. The bus driver and the ten children on board the bus were killed. According to local lore, since then the spirits of the dead children keep watch at the site and prevent others from suffering the same fate they did. They will push any stalled vehicle out of harm's way. Nearby streets are named in memory of those children.

That's the most frequently told version of the story, sometimes with slight alterations. The decade could be the 1940s or the 1950s. No one is quite sure. The time of the accident varies from early morning—and a rainy one at that—when the bus would have been delivering the students to school, to late afternoon when the youngsters were returning from an after-school outing. Sometimes the students are young, elementary school children ranging from 7 to 11 years. Sometimes they are teenagers. Sometimes there are survivors: the bus driver or even some of the children. In at least one version the bus driver is a woman—a nun, actually.

The nun story is recorded in *Weird Texas*, a compilation of legends put together by Wesley Treat, Heather Shades, and Rob Riggs. In that account the bus full of children is returning from a class outing in the country. It is late and dark, and the children are asleep. The bus stalls on the tracks. The nun, who is the children's teacher and the driver of the bus, does not wake them as she tries to restart the bus. That's when she hears the train, running with no lights and, as it turns out, with the engineer asleep at the controls. One last effort to start the bus fails, and it is hit and ripped in two by the speeding train, with the front half of the bus thrown from the tracks. The nun escapes unhurt but is forever haunted by the memory of the crash and the deaths of the young people in her care.

There is an epilogue of sorts to that story. The nun is so grief stricken she decides to take her own life by parking her car on the same tracks and waiting in the dark for the approach of the train. When she hears it in the distance, she begins to hear something else: the voices of children. The voices get louder, and her car begins to move, to lurch forward as if pushed out of the way, just before the train would have struck it. When her vehicle rolls to a stop, she gets out and sees children's handprints all over her car. Feeling she was spared for some purpose, perhaps, she goes on to establish an orphanage and spends the rest of her life caring for children. When she dies, some at her funeral claim to hear voices of children at play and the laughter of one adult.

Children of the Tracks railroad tracks
Donald Ray Boyd, photographer

Another story also focuses on the guilt experienced by the bus driver, in this case a male, who survives, this time by leaping to safety before the train collides with the bus. Even some twenty-five years later, the driver, now living in Chicago and working as a school custodian, cannot escape the memory and the lingering nightmares. Newspapers and television programs continue to recount the particulars of the tragedy and speculate about the truth of the details even a quarter of a century later in author Tim Tingle's adapted version. Tingle even gives the driver a name, Alba, and counts the number of children who perished at twenty-three. Some of the children have names too, Hispanic-sounding names: Roberto, Teresita, Adela, Stefán, Ignacio, Rebecca. In this scenario the children return to haunt not only the tracks in San Antonio but Alba's room in Chicago, crying out to Alba, "Don't go!" as he recalls opening the door to the bus, jumping out, and fleeing.

Meanwhile, back in San Antonio, the story continues, a woman named Hortencia wakens her ghostly grandson, Roberto, every school day morning and walks with him to the bus stop. Her neighbors watch the ritual from behind their lace curtains, shake their heads, and say a little prayer for the poor deluded woman. In this version of the story, Tingle has Hortencia and Alba, who has returned to the scene of the wreck, meet at the bus stop and experience a moment of resolution and forgiveness. The "Don't go!" voiced by the children takes on new meaning for Alba: "You do not have to run from us. . . . We are your friends." Clearly, "what if" possibilities of the story can take on many forms in the creative minds of storytellers. The paranormal claims are included by Tingle only as a kind of postscript: "It is said the children still guard the railroad tracks."

So what, if anything, is true about what is generally labeled "the children of the tracks"? Like many other researchers, Docia Schultz Williams, a storyteller and recorder of Texas ghost stories, says she has tried but failed to find any records in libraries and newspaper files that might help her sort out and substantiate the details of the train-bus wreck. She even talked to "a couple of elderly Southern Pacific Railroad men, and they said they vaguely recalled hearing about such an accident but could recall no details." The truth of the matter is that no one so far has been able to document the account of the wreck, though apparently many have tried. So here's what may have happened, according to the Snopes.com website, which bills itself as "the definitive Internet reference source for urban legends, folklore, myths, rumors, and misinformation." The Snopes researchers offer this possible explanation:

> *In December 1938, in Salt Lake City, Utah, twenty-six children, aged 12 to 18, lost their lives when the school bus they'd been travelling in stalled on the tracks and was struck by a freight train. No similar accident took place in San Antonio, but in 1938 that city was subjected to about ten days' worth of gruesomely detailed coverage in its local newspaper of the Salt Lake City crash, memory of which afterwards served to convince later generations the tragedy had taken place locally.*

The Utah tragedy is documented in great detail, both in archived newspaper accounts from 1938 and in more recent articles and broadcast reports published in 2013 when the seventy-fifth anniversary of the crash was the occasion for unveiling a permanent memorial to those who died. The bus driver and twenty-three Jordan High School students lost their lives in the midst of a blizzard when the driver failed to see through the snow and fog the approach of a Denver and Rio Grande Western freight train pulling as many as fifty or maybe even eighty cars. The train crew did see the bus pull onto the tracks and applied brakes, but they were too late to avoid the accident. Fifteen students survived but were left with "serious physical injuries and emotional scars," according to an article in the *Salt Lake Tribune*. The South Jordan community is about ten miles south of Salt Lake City. As a side note, in the wake of this accident came railroad crossing laws, mechanized crossing arms, and national regulations still in place today.

There is no mechanized crossing arm at the alleged site of a bus-train wreck in San Antonio, only the familiar "X" railroad crossing sign. And how and why that particular crossing has been singled out is part of the mystery, but it has been consistently noted as the specific location in each of the variants of the "children of the tracks" story. It is in a nondescript part of town where Villamain Road becomes Shane Road, and at times—particularly around Halloween—there is some congestion at the site as drivers wait in line to see for themselves if the place is haunted by the spirits of dead children. Some stop on the tracks themselves; others stop up to thirty to fifty yards away, headed west.

The true believers offer testimonies about what happens next. One report comes from Brenda Pacheco, quoted by Stephen Wagner, a self-described paranormal phenomena expert. Pacheco had reported her experience on a website sponsored by the *San Antonio Express-News* and a local television station. "I put my car in neutral," Pacheco writes, "took my foot off the pedals and the car moved! It moved quickly toward the tracks, up over the bump and down the other side, well out of harm's way!" She repeated the experiment, going "up and over the hill again." This time, she says, "I got out, and there were several little handprints, not only on the back of the car, but down the sides toward the back doors! And there was one big handprint on the side!" This larger handprint, she suggests, might have been that of the bus driver. "That's what we think," she concludes.

Now for some debunking. First of all, is the car really being pushed uphill? The myth busters say no. A SyFy network show, *Fact or Faked*, sent a team of researchers to San Antonio to test the legend, according to the RoadsideAmerica.com website, and left with the conclusion that the trees in the background at the scene cause an "optical illusion in regards to the 'angle' or direction you are looking as you are sitting behind the wheel." Furthermore, in his blog, Mark Louis Rybczyk, author of *San Antonio Uncovered*, says, "The road is actually a slight decline which causes your car to roll over the track. However, the horizon gives the impression that the car is actually being pushed uphill." More specifically, Wagner says that a surveyor has determined that the street surface is "actually at a 2 degree declination" as it approaches the railroad track crossing. The San Antonio story is likely just one of a whole subset of "gravity hill tales."

So what about the handprints? Most likely they are the prints of the vehicle's owner, say the skeptics. The baby powder (or sometimes flour or cornstarch) simply attaches to the oily residue left behind when a decidedly mortal person closes the trunk lid. This approach is similar to police detectives dusting for fingerprints.

Then there's that claim that the streets in the immediate area of the said-to-be-haunted tracks are named for the children who died in the crash. It's true that the streets have names such as Shane, Bobbie Allen, Cindy Sue, Laura Lee, Nancy Carole, and Richey Otis. There is even a spin-off story about Cindy Sue that follows the pattern of the vanishing hitchhiker legend. In this tale a woman is driving past the area late one night. She sees a little girl standing beside the road, so the woman stops and offers to take the little girl, who says her name is Cindy Sue, home. When they arrive at the little girl's home, Cindy Sue is reluctant to get out of the car. The woman approaches the house and speaks with the mother, who cries out, "No, this can't be. Cindy Sue is dead!" When they rush to the car, of course, Cindy Sue is gone. As she drives away, the woman notices the name of the street she is on is Cindy Sue Way.

Once again, however, there is an explanation about the street names. It's as simple as this: Apparently the developer of the neighborhood named the streets after his own very mortal children—or maybe it was his grandchildren.

Nevertheless, in spite of evidence to the contrary, visitors to the site continue to report strange goings-on. They report voices, specifically children's voices, cries, and laughter when no one is in sight. Some claim to have photographs of the area that include a ghostly image of a little girl or orbs supposed to be spirits. Some insist that the handprints on trunk lids and bumpers are definitely small and childlike, not the larger prints that would be left by adult drivers or passengers in the car. One variant cited by Snopes .com suggests that hoof prints appear among the handprints, as if "some form of tame demon" is assisting the dead children. With regard to the voices, at least, debunkers point out that they could come from a nearby playground or might even be the cries of peacocks in the area.

Stubbornly persistent in their views that something paranormal is going on at or near the tracks, individuals have offered detailed accounts meant to debunk the debunkers. One such report comes from an unnamed source writing to the Legends of America website. Having gone to the railroad tracks with friends one afternoon, the respondent says they had gone over the tracks several times themselves and then started chatting with some other visitors to the site. The visitors had already made the trip across the tracks once, but their guests, a man and wife from Mexico, didn't believe the legend and supposed the first driver had made the car roll. So the first driver got out and insisted that the Mexican visitor take the wheel for himself. He did.

Following instructions, he shut off the engine when the car, a big Lincoln Continental, was about five yards back from the tracks. The car began to roll. The man slammed on the brakes and even tried to put the transmission into "park," but still the car moved forward. "I've never seen anyone so terrified," the respondent says. "Once the car finally stopped, he jumped out, still screaming and shouting in Spanish, then demanded that his hosts take him back to his hotel, stating further that he was leaving and was *never* coming back!"

It may have been the same contributor who described going to the tracks in a 1968 Firebird convertible with a new parakeet in the car. "The bird had been chirping happily, until we staged the vehicle for the tracks, when suddenly his chirping was completely silenced. It wasn't until we left the area that he began to chirp again."

Another account of a car moving even though brakes were applied comes from Audra Sweet, quoted in *Weird Texas*:

> *My husband was driving our car with me riding shotgun and his sister in the back seat. We covered the car with baby powder and parked on the tracks. We shut the car off and put on the emergency brake and my husband pushed as hard as he could on the brakes. After a few seconds the car started rocking as if someone was pushing us from behind. My sister-in-law burst into tears and said, "Look!" I turned to look back at her and saw big and little handprints in the baby powder on the window next to her. The rocking continued all the while my husband had his feet on the brakes. Then the car rolled uphill as if we were driving, and then down away from the tracks to safety. It was an experience I will never forget.*

A comment from Steve R. Lawrence offers another slight challenge to the debunking on the Spookannie website. He claims that during his visit to the tracks, when the car eventually crosses over, "there is a strange sense of momentum" as the car goes up and over. A Yelp responder reports that the car radio "got super staticky and cut out" as the car approached the tracks.

While acknowledging that whether "there ever was an accident involving children on a school bus at this spot is open to serious question," Stephen Wagner says that "many people report other strange phenomena taking place there." One example is that of a man who was using a recording device at the tracks and "recorded an unexplained heartbeat." Another example reports a claim from a woman who says that instead of seeing handprints on the car she discovered "little blood droplets all over her trunk." A reader's comment on the Legends of America website agrees that "there *is* something psychic in the area." She lists her name as Myrene and speculates that "the spirits there go much farther back in history than the use of buses." And so it goes.

The stories continue in the oral tradition of folklore and in reports and investigations on popular television shows and in numerous newspapers and magazines. In 2015 the legend surfaced again in print on mysanantonio.com when the tracks were closed temporarily while railroad crews installed a sideline track that now runs parallel to the original, "supposedly haunted line." The construction was supposed to be completed by October 2015, just in time for Halloween. A spokesman for Union Pacific, Jeff DeGraff, said the ghost lore about the tracks "played no part in the design." As a cautionary note, he added, "The stories are something we are aware of. We will continue to educate people how terribly dangerous it is to stop on a train track. Hopefully it's something people will disregard instead of play into it."

Judging from the human interest in the legend so far, that's not likely to happen.

CHAPTER 12

The Legendary Sally Skull

So whatever happened to Sally Skull? Well, there are stories. One is that she was done in by husband number five. That would be Christof Horsdorff, or "Horsetrough," as some people called him. The manner of the alleged murder is pure conjecture, but the end is always the same: The two rode out from their Banquete ranch together one day in 1866; only one came back. All Horsdorff would say was that Sally "disappeared." Some of the speculation offered by others is more specific and graphic, usually to the effect that he blew off the top of her head with a shotgun and buried her in a shallow grave. A man named McDowell claimed some time later that he saw a boot sticking out of the ground and uncovered the body of a woman; but, even if that was true, no clear identification was made.

The motive? Money. Sally had freighted on the Cotton Road during the Civil War selling Texas-grown cotton to European buyers in Matamoros, Mexico, and returning with a horse's nosebag full of gold hanging from her saddle horn. Nevertheless, no proof of murder was offered, and Horsdorff was never charged. By 1868 he had moved north and remarried. Only one cryptic note in court records from 1867 in San Patricio County possibly alludes to Sally's disappearance. In a continuing suit filed against Sally and her fourth husband for reasons now unknown, court minutes conclude: "death of Defendant suggested."

Legends of murderous intent are not limited to stories about the disappearance of Sally herself. In fact, she may have been responsible for the disappearance of husband number two and/or three. Husband number one, Jesse Robinson, divorced her in 1843 after ten years of marriage and two children, Nancy and Albert. Eleven days later, Sally married George H. Scull, a gunsmith. The next year the two of them sold the last 400 acres she had inherited from her father along with livestock and Scull's gun maker's tools and farming implements. By 1849 Sally declared herself a single woman again and said Scull was deceased. She offered no further details.

Husband number three was John Doyle, whom Sally married in 1852, although she generally opted to keep the name of husband number two and change the spelling from Scull to Skull. By this time she was a successful horse trader and freighter operating out of the village of Banquete, about twenty miles west of Corpus Christi. Within three years she and Doyle had acquired 150 acres of land, livestock, and a wagon.

Then Doyle disappeared from the record too. In most of the stories about Sally's alleged murderous intent, he's her victim. She was a crack shot and habitually wore two pistols. One tale is that Doyle attempted to ambush her, but she returned fire when his first shot missed. She didn't miss in the ensuing duel. Another version has her and Doyle staying at a Corpus Christi hotel after dancing into the night at a fandango—a general term for dances, derived from the name of the lively Spanish dance it denotes. When Doyle couldn't rouse her the next morning, he poured a pitcher of water on her head. She came awake shooting, and down he went, although she later said she wouldn't have done it if she'd known it was him. Yet another fandango-related story says Doyle stopped at the whiskey barrel for one more drink and Sally pushed his head under, crying, "There, drink your fill!" until he drowned.

Or maybe he drowned the more conventional way—in a river. Yet another description of Doyle's possible demise has him approaching a swollen river either with a yoke of oxen aiming for a ferry or on horseback simply trying to ride his mount across the river on the rise, following orders from Sally. In either case he is swept away and drowned. Follow-up comments from Sally indicate regret on the one hand, indifference on the other. One report was that she said she would rather lose her best yoke of oxen than her man. The other was that she told her vaqueros not to bother searching for Doyle's body. "I don't give a damn about the body, but I sure would like to have the $40 in that money belt around it."

Whatever her fate or the fates of her five husbands, Sally certainly was a legend even in her own time. For some parents she served as a boogey woman. Frontier mothers sometimes threatened their children with "You'd better be good or Sally Skull will get you." Judging from her care and concern for her own children, however, that may be an ironic twist to her image. She and the children's father, Jesse Robinson, battled over custody of Nancy and Albert, not so much in the courts as in the matter of their education. Following the Robinsons' divorce and Sally's subsequent remarriage, Sally took the children to New Orleans and placed them in a convent school. Jesse followed, removed them, and put them in another convent school. Sally found them and enrolled them in yet another school. If legends are true, the feuding parents swapped the children back and forth several more times. Throughout, by all accounts, the persistent Sally remained a loving and devoted mother, sometimes indulgent and always affectionate. Reports are that even when her children were grown, Sally would make the effort to visit them during her trips on the Cotton Road.

Still, Sally's general reputation remained one that pictured her as a gun-toting, whip-lashing, hard-riding, rough-talking, no-nonsense pioneer, and that reputation began early, when her behavioral choices were no doubt influenced by her time and place. Born Sarah Jane Newman in Illinois, she moved to Texas with her family in 1823 when she was only six years old. They were among the first "Old Three Hundred" settlers in Stephen F. Austin's colony and were inhabiting an area along the Colorado River that the Comanches still considered to be part of their traditional hunting grounds. Sally likely inherited some of her combative tendencies from her mother, Rachel Rabb Newman, who managed to repel Comanche advances on at least two occasions. Once, when she spied a warrior's foot intruding under the cabin door, she raised a double-bit ax and brought it down to cut off his toes. Another time, when warriors tried to enter the cabin through the chimney, she set fire to a feather pillow and sent smoke and flames up the chimney.

A fairly young Sally reportedly showed the spunk that was to characterize her throughout her life when she, her sister, and her mother spied two Indians approaching their cabin. A neighbor man happened to be visiting, but when he saw the Indians, he pretended his gun was broken so he wouldn't have to challenge them. He said something like, "I wish I was two men; then I would fight those Indians." Sally's response was, "If you were one man, you would fight them. Give me that gun." Details of the outcome did not survive in the telling, but, clearly, Sally did survive.

Even beyond her early childhood encounters as a pioneer settler, Sally, as a young woman, experienced more than her share of history. She married her first husband when she was only sixteen. He was a man twice her age and a colorful character in his own right, a Texas Ranger and a soldier during the Texas Revolution. By the time the Alamo fell in 1836, she had a two-year-old daughter, and was no doubt caught up in the Runaway Scrape, the panicky exodus of Texans following the defeat of the Alamo defenders by the Mexican army. The great fear that provoked the exodus was that Mexican general Antonio López de Santa Anna, after his victory in San Antonio, would continue to lead his armies eastward in his attempted conquest of Texas. So those in the settlements gathered no more than a few of their possessions, abandoned their homes, and headed for Louisiana or Galveston. A young Texas Ranger, Noah Smithwick, later recalled the scenes he witnessed riding through the empty countryside:

> *The desolation of the country through which we passed beggars description. Houses were standing open, the beds*

unmade, the breakfast things still on the tables, pans of milk molding in the dairies. There were cribs full of corn, smoke houses full of bacon, yards full of chickens that ran after us for food, nests of eggs in every fence corner, young corn and garden truck rejoicing in the rain, cattle cropping luxuriant grass, hogs, fat and lazy, wallowing in the mud, all abandoned. Forlorn dogs roamed around the deserted homes, their doleful howls adding to the general sense of desolation. Hungry cats mewing to meet us rubbing their sides against our legs in token of welcome. Wagons were so scarce that it was impossible to remove household goods, many of the women and children, even, had to walk.

The corn and other garden vegetables may have rejoiced in the rain, but the fleeing settlers did not, for it was a cold rain that turned the roads into quagmires and made their journey all the more difficult. They had to endure not only the cold and the rain but hunger and disease. Many persons died along the way and were buried where they fell, but, once again, Sally survived that period, as did her child. Once the Texans, including Sally's husband, defeated the Mexican army at San Jacinto seven weeks after the fall of the Alamo, the refugees returned to their homes.

Years later, at the outbreak of the Civil War, Sally, now married to her fifth husband, Christof Horsdorff, began hauling Texas cotton to Mexico for shipment to Europe. Union naval forces had established a blockade along the Texas coast, attempting to shut down shipping exports and imports through Galveston and other Texas ports. Sally, already an experienced horse and cattle trader, likely saw opportunity. She could buy east Texas cotton for a few cents a pound and sell it in Matamoros, Mexico, for up to a dollar a pound. She went into business as a freighter. The Horsdorffs' ranch at Banquete was halfway along a stretch of the old Camino Real, later called the Cotton Road, running between the railhead at Alleytown and Matamoros, just across the Rio Grande from Brownsville. Sally, who spoke fluent Spanish, knew the road well, having traveled it frequently to buy horses south of the border and then taking them to east Texas or, perhaps, even to New Orleans to sell. She bought a string of wagons and hired Mexican teamsters to handle them, now hauling bales along the Cotton Road. The back-haul brought European imports of guns, ammunition, medicine, coffee, shoes, clothing, and other goods vital to Texas residents and to the Confederate cause.

Descriptions of her have her wearing buckskin bloomers, riding astride her horse instead of side saddle, and sporting holstered six shooters. She often carried a bullwhip and was so proficient with it that she could snap the heads off flowers for practice and inflict real damage to a man's back or shoulders if he crossed her. Her skill with a rifle would qualify her as a sharpshooter well before the time of Annie Oakley. She had penetrating blue eyes and fair skin roughened by exposure to sun and weather, even though she often wore a slatted sunbonnet. Her language was said to be as rough as any man's, and she was expert at cussing.

She registered her own brands, and never was anyone permitted to inspect or cut her herds. During her horse-trading days there were those who questioned her methods of acquiring her stock. Generally it was acknowledged that she paid for horses with the gold that she carried with her, but some stories suggested that she might have bypassed the legitimate purchase of animals and rounded them up by other means. According to Dan Kilgore, who wrote a biographical account of Skull:

One accusation was that after she visited the ranches of the neighborhood, raiding Lipan and Comanche Indians drove off the best horses which later turned up in her herds. Jealous wives spread the story that while she visited and made eyes at their men at the house, her vaqueros would be riding the pastures running off the horses.

Among her contemporaries was John S. "Rip" Ford, a Texas Ranger, who reported seeing her at the Lone Star Fair in Corpus Christi in May 1852. In his memoirs, years later, he wrote:

The last incident attracting the writer's attention occurred while he was at Kinney's Tank, wending his way home [from the fair]. He heard the report of a pistol, raised his eyes, saw a man falling to the ground, and a woman not far from him in the act of lowering a six-shooter. She was a noted character, named Sally Scull. She was famed as a rough fighter, and prudent men did not willingly provoke her in a row. It was understood that she was justified in what she did on this occasion; having acted in self-defense.

Another likely allusion to her was recorded by a European tourist who overheard a conversation in a Victoria hotel in 1853:

The conversation of these bravos drew my attention to the female character of the Texas frontier life, and, on inquiry, I heard the following particulars. They were speaking of a North American amazon, a perfect female desperado, who from inclination has chosen for her residence the wild border-country on the Rio Grande. She can handle a revolver and bowie-knife like the most reckless and skillful man; she appears at dances (fandangos) thus armed, and has even shot several men at merry-makings. She carries on the trade of a cattle-dealer, and common carrier. She drives wild horses from the prairie to market, and takes her oxen-waggon [sic], alone, through the ill-reputed country between Corpus Christi and the Rio Grande.

Two other anecdotes are without attribution but are frequently told by those who would try to chronicle Sally's life. Both illustrate her independent and contentious nature. In the first, a stranger drew her wrath by making some insulting remarks about her, behind her back. She found out about them and then found him, telling him to "dance" as she fired her six-shooters at his fast moving boots. In another instance she confronted a freighter who owed her money. This time she grabbed an ax and threatened to chop the front wheels off of every wagon he owned if he didn't pay. Word is he paid.

Aside from the few written notes provided by some of her contemporaries such as Ford and the European tourist, most of Sally's legend has been perpetuated by tales told orally with heavy doses of speculation and likely embellishments. Because of courthouse fires and other misfortunes, few documents remain to verify or refute some of the claims about her. Still, a fairly consistent portrait emerges, even with suspected exaggerations. And apparently she was known to enjoy some of the social pleasures of frontier life: she loved to dance at fandangos. She was also known to sit in on games of draw poker. Hers was a colorful and sometimes paradoxical life.

For those who prefer happier endings, by the way, there are even stories that Sally was not murdered after all. Folklorist and writer Dan Kilgore says he once visited with two men born in the 1870s—well after Sally's supposed demise—who claimed they had seen Sally when they were children. One of them, a man from Beeville, "recalled that he and his brother would throw silver dollars in the air for her to shoot holes in them with her pistols. The boys would beg her for the perforated coin but she would say, 'No, I will take it home, patch it up and use it.'" Other, less substantiated theories suggest that perhaps she moved west and lived with a Newman relative near El Paso. That story persisted in at least one branch of the Newman family, according to Kilgore. Other reported sightings place her around Goliad or Halletsville in the 1870s.

Whatever the truth about her death, it can certainly be said that Sally Skull lives on in the imagination of writers, storytellers, and historians. Portrayed by actress O-Lan Jones, she even appears in one episode of the television mini-series adaptation of Larry McMurtry's *Lonesome Dove*. In 1964 the State of Texas erected a historical marker in her honor two miles north of Refugio at the intersection of two highways. It has now been moved to the front lawn of the Refugio County courthouse.

Sally Scull/Skull historical marker

DONALD RAY BOYD, PHOTOGRAPHER

CHAPTER 13

The Hanging of Chipita Rodriguez

I n February 1998 the folks around San Patricio waited and watched to see if the spirit of Chipita Rodriguez would stir. She had walked before, they said, anytime a woman was sentenced to die in the State of Texas. And Karla Faye Tucker was on death row.

If Chipita appeared, it would likely be down along the Aransas or the Nueces River. She would be wearing a white dress with blue trim—and a frayed noose around her neck. She would be wailing and moaning and still crying out, "*No soy culpable*" (I am not guilty).

This is her story: In 1863 she had a cabin that served as an inn of sorts along the Cotton Road, the old Camino Real, a few miles north of San Patricio. Because Union warships had blockaded Southern ports during the Civil War, cotton was hauled overland across south Texas on that road and sold in Matamoros on the Mexican side of the Rio Grande to help raise money for the Confederate cause. Others also traveled the road, from just east of Houston south to the Confederacy's back door. One of those travelers was John Savage, a horse trader, and apparently a pretty good one. He had $600 in gold in his saddlebags from the sale of horses to the Confederate army. Because he wouldn't be making it to the Rio Grande by nightfall, he stopped at Chipita's inn. She offered him little more than a hot meal for supper and a cot on her lean-to porch on which to spread his bedroll.

The next morning he was gone, but not very far. His body, hacked to death by Chipita's wood-chopping ax, was found stuffed into a burlap bag. It was drifting in the Aransas River not far from Chipita's cabin. His saddlebags, still full of gold, were nearby.

Chipita was arrested and charged with murder. "*No soy culpable,*" she said. She was silent all through her trial, except to repeat, "*No soy culpable.*" The jury found her guilty but recommended mercy. An itinerant judge named Benjamin F. Neal, however, ordered her to be executed. She waited in the San Patricio lean-to jail, secured with leg irons and chains to the back wall of the courthouse. Townspeople brought her food and corn-husk cigarettes. Schoolchildren shared their cookies. A local woman brought Chipita a white mull dress so that she would have something decent to wear to her hanging.

Another woman fought off the deputy sheriff with a stick when he came to borrow her sturdy new wagon to take Chipita and her wooden coffin to the hanging tree. The deputy had to go elsewhere to secure his transportation. Chipita, dressed as if for a party and still in chains, sat on her coffin in a two-wheeled cart and smoked a corn-husk cigarette as the death wagon moved through town and out to the Nueces River on a dreary, misty, stormy afternoon, Friday the 13th in November 1863. Ordered to stand on top of the coffin while the hangman placed the noose around her neck, she refused a blindfold and looked out at the crowd assembled, saying only these last words: "*No soy culpable.*"

The hangman struck the oxen hitched to the cart, and they lurched forward. Chipita swung free and died—or did she?

The hangman wrestled the heavy coffin into a hastily dug shallow grave right there under the tree, placed Chipita's body in the coffin, put the lid in place, and shoveled back the dirt. One bystander swore he heard a moan coming from the coffin, and Chipita's words stayed with him: "*No soy culpable.*"

On his way to church the next Sunday, the sheriff who arrested Chipita turned around and went home when, he said, he saw the Devil sitting on a fence. Before long, others reported seeing a ghostly figure, a restless spirit, haunting the river bottoms. It was Chipita, they said, buried without a funeral or a wake and still protesting her innocence.

Since then, her ghost has shown up, the locals say, whenever any other Texas woman is condemned to die. Four times she stirred, and four women avoided execution. If she walked on the night of February 2, 1998, however, it did no good. Karla Faye Tucker, also accused of an ax murder, died by lethal injection.

So did Chipita Rodriguez kill John Savage for his money? The one piece of circumstantial evidence was the ax. It did belong to Chipita. But if she wanted the money, why was it still in the saddlebags? Another suspect, Juan Silvera, was arrested with Chipita as an accomplice. She would, after all, need help to dispose of Savage's body. Silvera was sentenced to five years in prison.

And why did Chipita offer no explanation or alibi in her own defense? Speculation among those who thought her innocent was that she was covering up for someone else, possibly Silvera, who some believed was her illegitimate son.

Little was known, really, about Chipita Rodriguez. Her real name may have been Josefa, according to researcher Marylyn Underwood, and she likely moved from Mexico to San Patricio de Hibernia in Texas with her father, Pedro. He was said to be fleeing from Antonio López de Santa Anna, best known for leading the Mexican army in the battle at the Alamo. After her father's death Chipita continued to operate the inn he had established on the Aransas River. Rumor was that she took up with a cowboy and bore him a son, subsequently taken away by the father when he abandoned Chipita and disappeared. How Juan Silvera figures into this relationship is not entirely clear.

Was he, in fact, Chipita's illegitimate son come home, or merely a hired man or a neighbor? His status as son is brought up in "Shadows on the Nueces," an epic poem written by Rachel Bluntzer Hebert. Its premise is that Kate McCumber, the woman who rebuffed the deputy seeking to borrow a wagon, finally told her daughter the story she had heard from Chipita the day before the hanging forty years earlier. According to the lines of the epic, Kate, who had befriended Chipita and visited her in her court- house cell, said that not one, but two men had arrived at Chipita's inn that fateful night in August 1863. After Savage was settled in, it seems that "another came to bother," and Chipita thought she recognized in him "the form of father," the likeness of that cowboy who had abandoned her. Could this be her long-lost son? "Was it clearly apparition / Or simply was it mother's intuition?"

Chipita said she had gone for a walk just before dark that evening and saw, as she was returning, her son kill Savage, take his horse, and ride away. Deserted again, she was left with a body and no alibi. Her first impulse was to hide the body. "Then she'd think what she must say." She enlisted the help of Juan Chiquito, the poem says. He was a neighbor, perhaps, "who was camping on the bend." The Spanish word *chiquito*, by the way, means "very small" and may have been a descriptive term rather than a surname. So this same Juan could be Juan Silvera. He came, and together they "lugged the sack to the river," thus attempting to hide the crime and, in Chipita's case, helping the real murderer escape.

Her refusal to say anything more at her trial than "*No soy culpable*" sealed Chipita's fate. The women of the town rallied to at least make her as comfortable and presentable as they could. They brought warm water to the jail so that Chipita could wash, and they "brushed and neatly braided / All her twisted, crow-black hair." Eliza Sullivan donated her daughter Rachel's fine blue-trimmed white dress, a favorite, according to Rachel's great-granddaughter, Mary Margaret Campbell, for Chipita to wear.

Kate McCumber said Chipita made her promise "Never to divulge her secret / Until the years had brewed a potion / Which had quieted all emotion." Supposedly McCumber's story, once she felt free to tell it, was passed down for years by family members before Hebert finally wrote her poem. Hebert's niece, Geraldine McGloin, says that her aunt took some poetic license, to be sure, but that the poem is based on the stories that circulated among local residents and on what court documents were available.

Whether this account is entirely true or not, there are plenty of reasons to question the court's verdict in Chipita's case. Because some of the archival records were destroyed in a courthouse fire and others in a flood, documentation is incomplete, but clearly the trial and execution were hastily carried out. Savage was murdered on August 23, 1863. Chipita and Juan were taken into custody and held in San Patricio. Chipita was indicted on October 7, tried on October 9, convicted, and sentenced to death on October 10—all that in the space of four days. There was no appeal.

The trial itself was irregular, to say the least. The sheriff who arrested Chipita, William Means, sat as foreman on the grand jury. Two members of his family also served. There was no jury panel as such for the trial. Instead, people were simply rounded up by the sheriff, resulting in what was quite possibly a "stacked" jury. At least three members of the grand jury also served on the trial jury. Several members of both juries had been indicted for felonies themselves, one of them for murder. Chipita had little in the way of defense counsel.

Still, even though the jury found her guilty on what testimony was presented, they recommended mercy "on account of her old age and the circumstantial evidence against her," according to the minutes of the district court. Chipita was apparently one of those aging yet ageless women who could have been anywhere between sixty and ninety. An unrelenting judge for the Fourteenth District Court, Benjamin F. Neal, ignored the jury's plea for leniency, however, and ordered her execution. He offered no explanation why.

At least one theory about the rush to judgment in Chipita's case has nothing to do with the murder. It has to do with war and politics. The Civil War at that time was going badly for the Confederates, and emotions ran high. Some in the area feared that Union forces would come ashore from the Gulf of Mexico any day. Earlier in the war Neal himself had commanded an artillery unit assigned to defend Corpus Christi, but his record was less than stellar. A little over a year before Chipita's trial, he had retreated from his post, withdrawing his company of soldiers from Mustang Island and yielding it and another nearby island to Union forces. A Confederate major complained that Neal had acted "with cowardice and indecorum." The following year Neal resigned his command, having been elected judge of the Fourteenth District. Marylyn Underwood says that some sources indicate that Chipita was suspected of having been "involved in gathering information to influence the state's decision about which side to take in the Civil War and was framed as a political act."

San Patricio County historian Keith Guthrie told an Associated Press writer, "I think it's true that the jury didn't believe she did the crime but they believed she knew who did." Guthrie said the foreman of the trial jury, Owen Gaffney, "passed down the word through his descendants that they gave her the harsh penalty to see if she wouldn't say who killed him [Savage]. All she ever said was 'not guilty' in Spanish."

Among the only remaining official records of the case are the minutes of the district court listing by name two attorneys for the prosecution and eleven men on the jury but mentioning only "their counsel" for the defendants. Chipita (sometimes spelled Chepita) and Juan had the arraignment and indictment read to them. They pleaded not guilty, and the jury heard the evidence against them before returning their verdict. The jury found Chipita guilty of murder in the first degree and Juan guilty of murder in the second degree and for him "assessed the penalty of five years confinement in the penitentiary." Follow-up documents note that "there was no motion for a new trial and no motion in arrest of judgment" in Juan's case and that "the motion for a new trial" was "withdrawn by the defendant counsel" in Chipita's case. Therefore, Juan's sentence of five years "at hard labor" was final, as was Chipita's sentence. On Friday, November 13, 1863, she was to "be taken to the place of execution and there between the hour of eleven o'clock and sunset . . . be executed according to the law by hanging by the neck until she be dead."

The only trees tall enough and strong enough to serve the hangman were down by the river. A popular notion is that the hanging tree was a mesquite, but that is unlikely, according to Garrett Klatt and Pat Conlan, county residents, who pointed out that mesquite trees didn't appear in the area until they were spread during King Ranch cattle drives after the Civil War. Whatever the tree was, it is gone now, and even the depression in the ground once pointed to as the site has disappeared after years of flooding and erosion. Because Chipita's grave was unmarked, no one is quite sure where her remains are either.

In the late 1970s several San Patricio–area residents began efforts to clear Chipita's name. Finally, State Senator Carlos Truan of Corpus Christi introduced a resolution, passed by the Senate and signed by Governor Mark White on July 13, 1985, that effectively pardoned Chipita. It declared, "Chipita Rodriguez, a 19th century inhabitant of San Patricio County and the only woman ever officially executed in the state of Texas, may have been wrongfully convicted of the crime for which she was executed." Lawmakers acknowledged that her trial appeared to violate state laws and called it "a rush to judgment that, even for 19th century Texas, was highly unusual."

This book cover sketch pictures Chipita's ox cart ride to her hanging.
<small>COURTESY OF MARY HEBERT MAURER</small>

Chipita was not, however, the only woman ever officially executed in the State of Texas up to that time. Apparently she was the third. The first was Jane Elkins, a slave convicted of murder and hanged in Dallas on May 27, 1853. The second, according to records cited by W. T. Block, was also a slave, a forty-year-old woman named Lucy. She was hanged for murder on the public gallows of Galveston Island on March 5, 1858. There are no widespread tales about the spirits of these other two women walking.

Chipita's spirit, however, figures prominently in a number of stories. Keith Guthrie says, "On any Friday 13th, but especially on November 13th [the anniversary of Chipita's execution] many people have felt or seen the ghost of Chipita Rodriguez" in the San Patricio area. Mostly, though, she is said to appear whenever a woman in Texas is convicted of murder and sentenced to die. Underwood lists the four times she walked and a woman avoided the hangman's noose or the electric chair. First there was a Fayette County woman due to be hanged after World War I. Guthrie says that Chipita "wandered the area for days, until the convicted woman died in her cell, and then Chipita's ghost disappeared." Then, according to Underwood, Chipita "moaned among the mesquites that line the Nueces River bottom" in the 1940s when Emma Oliver was condemned to die. When Oliver's sentence was commuted, Chipita "ceased her cries of anguish." She was "visible among the gnarled mesquites" again in 1959 when Maggie Morgan was facing death in the electric chair. Again the sentence was commuted, and again Chipita's ghost withdrew. She presumably came forward at least one more time in 1978 when Mary Lou Anderson was tried for murder, but Anderson's sentence was reduced when she testified against her accomplice.

Underwood surmises that Chipita, "disturbed by the circumstances of her own trial and execution, sees the awfulness of another woman's death," and that is what causes her specter to emerge. "Or, perhaps," Underwood says, "until her name is cleared, Chipita bemoans her fate." Interestingly enough, by 1998, when Karla Faye Tucker was executed, Chipita's name had been cleared by the resolution passed by the Sixty-ninth Legislature in 1985. There were no reported sightings of Chipita's ghost in 1998, so perhaps she can finally rest in peace.

However, as Guthrie points out, many of the first settlers in San Patricio County were "Irish-Catholic settlers brought directly from Ireland." It could be that Chipita will continue to appear to those still haunted by their own inherited sense of guilt, knowing that she should not have been put to death. To their way of thinking, her soul remains in limbo and will forever wander because she had no wake and was not buried in a cemetery. Underwood quotes a San Patricio resident as saying, "Could a more unholy or unnatural thing have happened to an Irish village?" Some even claim that the town has been cursed, "for never again did it thrive as before, and in 1893 the county seat was moved to nearby Sinton."

Certainly Chipita's legend lives on in print, through the oral tradition, and in music. In 1993 the University of Texas music department in Austin performed the opera *Chipita Rodriguez*, composed by professor Lawrence Weiner of Texas A&M University–Corpus Christi. Countless articles in newspapers, magazines, and journals have been published, a rash of them reiterating Chipita's story as Karla Faye Tucker's execution date approached.

Generally, anecdotal accounts of sightings—past ones and those recent enough to picture Chipita's ghost riding on the hood of a car—are still passed on from one person to another in the manner of folklore. Most often her spirit is described as drifting or gliding or moving like a shadow by trees along the Nueces River or along a path near the water. Sometimes she is merely the dark shape of a silhouette in the moonlight. Her audible protestations of her improper burial or of her innocence range in sound from a mournful sigh or a gentle sobbing to an unearthly wail or a sorrowful cry piercing the night.

One thing is sure: As long as the stories are told, some residents around San Patricio will continue to wait and watch and listen. For, as Underwood concludes, "legends are the stuff of the minds of the folk who believe or want to believe them."

CHAPTER 14

The Love Story of Frenchy McCormick

Mickey McCormick was a gambler who believed in luck, and he found himself a good-luck girl in Mobeetie, Texas. As long as she was standing beside him at the poker table, he won. Besides that, she was pretty and probably Irish to boot. She had black hair, blue eyes, and the figure of the dancing girl she was. The cowboys called her Frenchy, and she won his heart. So he brought her back with him to Tascosa, the Cowboy Capital of the Texas Panhandle.

The year was 1880. The town, a place for cowboys to "blow off a little steam," was young and thriving. It was earning a reputation as "the hardest place on the frontier" and had no law, as such. It did have a post office, a hotel, a restaurant, a doctor's office, a drugstore, a surveyor's office, a blacksmith shop, a millinery shop, two general supply stores, and two livery stables, one of which belonged to Mickey. It also had seven saloons and a Boot Hill cemetery.

Mickey operated gambling rooms behind one of the saloons, and soon Frenchy was dealing three-card monte, more a scam than a game of cards, similar to the con of a shell game. There in the back room she was the reigning belle, and she and Mickey entertained many a colorful character passing through, some legends in their own right: Billy the Kid, Pat Garrett, Bat Masterson.

Frenchy was not so popular with the womenfolk of Tascosa. As one woman put it, "The respectable element of the town had nothing to do with Frenchy and the other girls of her class." Another woman added, "Frenchy was pretty tough until they [she and Mickey] got married. I wouldn't have anything to do with her." She noted that not only was Frenchy quick to dance a jig, but she would also box with the men—and whip some of them.

Mickey and Frenchy (she called him Mack; he called her Elizabeth) married in 1881, and he built her a two-room adobe house by a twisted cottonwood tree on Atascosa Creek. Even the "respectable element of the town" admitted that although she still went to Mickey's dance and gambling hall, "she did not become one of the red light girls," and she stopped dealing monte. One of the good wives in town even remarked about Frenchy's "goodness and kindness" to others. People would see Frenchy carrying water to her neighbors "when they had typhoid fever and other times because she had good well water."

Then the railroad bypassed Tascosa in 1887, and the town began a steady decline. The McCormicks lost their business and subsisted on what Mickey earned hauling freight and what game he brought in as a hunter. Still, they stayed, devoted to each other and convinced that the town would come back some day. It didn't. By the time Mickey died in 1912, it was on its way to becoming a ghost town. Frenchy refused to leave, saying she would forever stay by her husband's grave site in the Casimero Romero family cemetery, established by early sheep-owning settlers and located only a short distance from her cabin. She could see her Mack's white marker every day by looking up the hill east from her well when she went to draw water. The final blow to the town came in 1915 when the county seat was moved to Vega. But Frenchy stayed on in the little adobe house with no electricity or running water.

For twenty-seven years she stayed, most of that time as the only living inhabitant left in Tascosa, other than the coyotes and the rattlesnakes. Abandoned buildings in the town began to crumble. Weeds grew in the streets. Only the stone courthouse stood strong against the elements. Frenchy endured blue northers and spring floods that cut her off and isolated her more than ever. She might go weeks without seeing or hearing another human being. She lived alone through the Depression and the blowing dirt storms of the Dust Bowl years.

She tried keeping dogs, which Mack had always loved. But the rattlesnakes got them, every one. Finally the rattlesnakes denned up right under the foundation of the adobe. She even killed one inside the house. Other wild things roamed about, and her good well was caving in. Friends urged her to move to safer, more comfortable quarters. "I'll stay with my Mack," she said. "I want to be buried by his side."

Finally, in 1939, at age eighty-seven, in frail health, and almost deaf, she was persuaded to move to nearby Channing and live with a friend, but only on condition that she be brought back to Tascosa after her death. She died two years later in January 1941.

It would have been less expensive for the county to bury her there in Channing, but a promise is a promise. So on a bitterly cold and windy winter's day, her funeral cortege made its way to Old Tascosa, past the Boot Hill cemetery, past the tumbledown adobe in which Frenchy had lived for almost sixty years, past the stone courthouse that now housed underprivileged boys in the newly established Cal Farley's Boys Ranch, and up a slope to the Romero graveyard. There a small choir from Boys Ranch sang "Home on the Range," and Frenchy, the "last Girl of the Golden West," was laid to rest at last beside her beloved Mack.

But the mystery of who she was, exactly, and where she came from was never entirely solved. "No one will find out who I am," she had said, except maybe Mickey, and he wasn't telling. For that matter, not much is known about Mickey's past either.

Judging from two documents, Frenchy's real name was Elizabeth McGraw. That's the name she gave for her marriage license in 1881 and again fifty-six years later when she applied for old-age assistance from the county. She said she was born in 1852 somewhere near Baton Rouge, Louisiana. Despite her nickname, she was likely of Irish descent.

From there the rest is conjecture, up until the time she met Mickey. One story says that after her mother died, Frenchy accompanied her father up the Mississippi on a steamboat to St. Louis. Her father did not approve of her love for dancing, especially in public on the burlesque stage and in the Benedict Bar in St. Louis. He threatened to put a stop to it. They quarreled, and she caught a stagecoach for Dodge City, Kansas, to perform in the dance halls there.

Another version is that she ran away from a convent school in Baton Rouge as a teenager in the company of a man who abandoned her. Either way, once she was in Dodge City, she took on her new identity as Frenchy after a cowboy started calling her that because she was from Louisiana and spoke French. She began to hear stories about the Texas Panhandle to the south, populated with cowboys and buffalo hunters. And there would be soldiers in Mobeetie, the first town established in the Panhandle, near Fort Elliott.

Frenchy McCormick arrived in Tascosa with a mysterious past.
Cal Farley's Boys Ranch

So, stories say, she packed all her satin slippers, her fancy dance dresses, her plumes, her beads, and her bangles and caught the stage for Texas. There she met Mickey, marking the beginning of their legendary love story. "Mack and I discussed the fact that we had lived somewhat on the seamy side," she would say later in her life, "and then he took both my hands in his and we pledged to stick to each other and to the town of Tascosa." However, it wasn't until Scotty Wilson, bartender and justice of the peace, got the first book of marriage licenses in newly formed Oldham County that Mickey and Frenchy were married. Wilson is said to have rounded up all the cowboys and gamblers who had paired up with dance hall girls and demanded that they legalize their unions by buying licenses and getting married. Mickey and Frenchy were among those who did. Later they had their marriage blessed by a Catholic priest.

Frenchy's status in Tascosa was a bit less than solid: Although some considered her a "respected citizen," the "solid citizenry" of the town conspicuously omitted her name from invitation lists for social functions. Her presence at the gaming tables did not escape notice, especially in her early years in Tascosa. J. Evetts Haley gleaned this description from early settlers passing through the town, among them the well-known rancher Charles Goodnight: "A little woman called 'Frenchy,' whose past rested safely among the unwritten biographies of Creole New Orleans, sat before a table and dealt the Mexican game [probably monte] with graceful efficiency." Haley and his sources are not the only ones to assume, possibly because of her nickname, that Frenchy was Creole rather than Irish and from New Orleans rather than Baton Rouge.

And Mickey was not the only one with a superstitious bent. If he thought his luck was better when Frenchy was beside him, she thought it was likely to disappear when any other woman was in the room. If that seemed to be happening, she would order the woman out, running her off forcibly if necessary.

That Frenchy was well educated, or at least had an above-average education, was generally accepted, and she was credited with having "a certain refinement." Her handwriting was a beautiful script. Although she professed to be Catholic, she did not go to church, saying at one point, "It might be out of place for me to go into the Lord's house."

The longer she stayed in the ghost town that Tascosa became, the more of a curiosity and an enigma she became. With no modern conveniences, she managed somehow to get along even as she aged. Oldham County authorities sent someone once a week to deliver food, coal, and kerosene. Newspaper reporters, historians, and museum curators requested interviews and aspired to catalog the papers and possessions she had locked away in trunks. According to researchers Pauline Durrett Robertson and R. L. Robertson, "She fought off two men, ostensibly from a college in Tennessee," who "had ripped open her trunk in the adobe house and were ransacking it when friends of Frenchy happened to drive up." Although she would grant interviews, Frenchy stopped talking when anyone questioned her about her past.

She was still sociable, however, as a story told by a onetime student at Old Tascosa indicates. Even though only Frenchy remained as a resident in the town itself, a dozen or so children from area farms and ranches and the children of workers in a nearby gravel pit continued to come to the schoolhouse at Old Tascosa, even into the 1930s. Casandra Firman has passed on a story told to her by her mother, Quintille, who was one of those students. In December 1931 the students and their teacher, Mrs. Talley, were in the school making preparations for a Christmas pageant to be presented that afternoon. Not only parents but also residents from a five-mile radius had been invited. Even if everyone came, however, there would be only a couple of dozen people.

Then it started to snow. The wind began to blow, and soon a blinding blizzard was raging. Even though the children and their teacher were safe and relatively warm if they stayed close to the potbellied stove in the schoolhouse, they knew no one could make it through the storm to watch their pageant. And the expected cookies and other sweets wouldn't make it either. At the height of their disappointment, one of the boys looked out the window and saw a figure coming through the snow. It was a woman, steadying herself with a cane and carrying a bundle. Two boys were dispatched to help her in, and the teacher introduced her as Mrs. McCormick. Frenchy McCormick was the only guest who made it to see the pageant that day, and she even brought some little cakes.

"Children," Mrs. Talley said, "our show must be especially good. Mrs. McCormick was once on the stage herself. She was a famous performer, and now we will perform for her." And they did. Years later Quintille still remembered singing for "the Belle of Old Tascosa."

The Robertsons learned from Lona Blackwell, the woman in Channing with whom Frenchy stayed during her last two years, and from a renter, Mrs. Hunnicutt, that Frenchy was "active and perky" up until the end. "Although she couldn't hear well, she was jolly and had a lot of company." Comfortable and happy as she appeared to be, however, "she often reminded us that she was only visiting in Channing; her home was in Tascosa."

At one point, two women from Louisiana saw Frenchy's photograph in a Fort Worth newspaper. They contacted Frenchy, convinced that she was a long-lost relative who had run away from home six or seven decades earlier. They sent her gifts and pictures and invited her to make her home with them for the rest of her life, but she expressed little interest. "If they will come to see me," she said, "I'll talk to them and see if we can get it straightened out." She still wasn't talking about her past, and she had no intention of going anywhere very far from Tascosa.

She continued to say that Tascosa would come back someday. "It's a wonderful town. The people all over the world will know about Tascosa." Her words seemed a distant echo of those printed in the *Tascosa Pioneer*, the frontier newspaper begun in 1886 by an ambitious young editor named Charles F. Randolph. Remarkably, copies of the *Pioneer* have survived, and they show that during the five years of the newspaper's existence Randolph was a tireless booster of the town. In its first issue, Randolph said, "The *Tascosa Pioneer* tips its beaver to the good people of the great Texas Panhandle on this fair June morning, and settles down to business, we can only hope, as one of the permanent institutions of the section." In 1887 Randolph still thought the railroad would come through Tascosa: "Doubts and uncertainties are dissolved like morning mists! And the little city has only to go on to greatness!" In that same year he noted that the Panhandle had seven newspapers, each claiming that its town was "the present and prospective metropolis," but, he said, "the rest need only settle among themselves the question of second place, for Tascosa will inevitably rank first. Evidences of that fact accumulate every day."

After the Fort Worth & Denver City Railroad bypassed Tascosa, Randolph ultimately accepted the inevitable, closed the *Pioneer*, and moved on to edit other newspapers in Texas. Only Frenchy kept her faith in the resurgence of Tascosa, and, in a way, her faith was rewarded. In 1939, the same year she moved out of her adobe and into Channing with Lona Blackwell, rancher Julian Bivins, who now owned the remains of Tascosa as part of his ranch, donated the old courthouse and the town's land to an organization working on behalf of underprivileged boys. Under the leadership of Cal Farley, Boys Ranch was established, beginning with nine boys living with houseparents in the courthouse.

Farley famously said and believed that all these neglected boys needed was "a shirttail to hang on to." Over the years more boys came, many more. They learned lessons in school and skills through their chores, for which they received an allowance. Under supervision they built sturdy, handsome buildings where once adobes stood. They played instruments in a band and sang in a choir. They played sports and competed each Labor Day weekend in the Boys Ranch Rodeo.

Before his death in 1967, Farley had realized his dream of providing a home for "the bottom ten per cent of America's youth," many of them just a step away from the reformatory. With slogans such as "It's where you're going that counts" and "It's easy to smile when someone cares," Farley took in sometimes belligerent and uncooperative boys and gave them an opportunity to become productive, useful citizens. He said, "The wildest colts make the best horses if properly trained."

Today Cal Farley's Boys Ranch advertises itself as "one of America's largest privately funded child and family service providers specializing in both residential and community-based services at no cost to the families of children in our care." Its campus has grown to resemble a small city. Currently, twenty-eight homes provide living and sleeping quarters for boys and now girls, housing approximately ten to twelve children each. The old courthouse is now the Julian Bivins Museum, where some of Frenchy McCormick's possessions are on display. The Oldham County schoolhouse, where the Christmas pageant took place, educated the first boys at the Ranch and was restored in the 1990s. It is currently used for special functions. The Boot Hill cemetery, begun in the 1880s following a gun battle, overlooks Boys Ranch and is a popular tourist attraction. Boys Ranch Chapel, dedicated in 1973, sits on a hill and provides a central focus for the campus. As a self-contained community, Boys Ranch has its own post office, medical facilities, parks, and sports fields—just like any other Texas Panhandle town.

Frenchy knew about the beginnings of Boys Ranch and likely was glad that it brought new life to Old Tascosa. And now the unique town that Old Tascosa has become is known all over the world. The boys at the Ranch know about Frenchy too. Her story is briefly told in the Boys Ranch brochure. Although her house is gone now, the adobe having crumbled away, the twisted-trunk cottonwood tree by Atascosa Creek still stands to mark the spot where she lived as "a perfect example of love and fidelity." That's what the Catholic priest said about her during her funeral rites. Six boys from the Ranch formed the small choir that sang at her burial. Later, alumni from Boys Ranch raised money to erect a marble headstone for her in the Romero cemetery.

That cemetery is not on Boys Ranch property. It is on ranch land to the east. Hardly anyone goes there anymore, and the road to it is rutted and poorly maintained. The graveyard is "ramshackle and overgrown," but two white marble markers, side by side, are still visible to those who seek them out, reminders of times past and of a legendary Panhandle love story.

BIBLIOGRAPHY

JEAN LAFITTE'S TREASURES

Abney, A. H. *Life and Adventures of L. D. Lafferty.* New York: Goodspeed, 1875.

Beazley, Julia. "The Uneasy Ghost of Lafitte." In *Legends of Texas,* edited by J. Frank Dobie, 185–189. Hatboro, PA: Folklore Associates, [1924] 1964.

Cartwright, Gary. *Galveston: A History of the Island.* New York: Atheneum, 1991.

Dobie, J. Frank. *Coronado's Children: Tales of Lost Mines and Buried Treasures of the Southwest.* Austin: University of Texas Press, [1930] 1978.

Fowler, Zinita. *Ghost Stories of Old Texas II.* Austin, TX: Eakin, 1992.

———. *Ghost Stories of Old Texas III.* Austin, TX: Eakin, 1995.

Gonzalez, Catherine Troxell. *Lafitte: The Terror of the Gulf.* Austin, TX: Eakin, 1981.

Jameson, W. C. *Buried Treasures of Texas.* Little Rock, AR: August House, 1991.

"Jean Lafitte: Buccaneer of Barataria Bay." In *Reader's Digest American Folklore and Legend,* 80–81. Pleasantville, NY: Reader's Digest Association, 1978.

"Jean Lafitte: Gulf Coast Pirate and Privateer." http://jeanlafitte .net.

Kemah Historical Society. "The Legend of Jean Lafitte." www .kemahhistoricalsociety.net/legendl.html.

"Saga of Our Pirate." Historical Brochure: A Record of the Celebration of the Seventy-fifth Anniversary of the Founding of La Porte, Texas, 1964.

Schlosser, S. E. *Spooky Southwest: Tales of Hauntings, Strange Happenings, and Other Local Lore.* Guilford, CT: Globe Pequot, 2004.

Son of the South. "The History of Texas: Jean Lafitte." www .sonofthesouth.net/texas/jean-lafitte.htm.

Syers, William Edward. *Off the Beaten Trail.* Waco, TX: Texian, 1971.

Warren, Harris Gaylord. "Jean Lafitte." *Handbook of Texas Online,* www.tshaonline.org/handbook/online/articles/LL/fla12.html.

THE LOST SAN SABA MINE

Dobie, J. Frank. "The Legend of the San Saba or Bowie Mine." In *Legends of Texas*, edited by J. Frank Dobie, 12–20. Hatboro: PA: Folklore Associates, [1924] 1964.

———. *Coronado's Children: Tales of Lost Mines and Buried Treasures of the Southwest.* Austin: University of Texas Press, [1930] 1978.

Eckhardt, C. F. *The Lost San Saba Mines.* Austin: Texas Monthly Press, 1982.

———. *Texas Tales Your Teacher Never Told You.* Plano, TX: Wordware, 1991.

Estill, Julia. "Lost Mines of the Llano and San Saba." In *Legends of Texas*, edited by J. Frank Dobie, 24–27. Hatboro: PA: Folklore Associates, [1924] 1964.

Harmes, Joseph, and Bob Stewart. "Storming the Alamo." *People*, May 2, 1994. www.people.com/people/archive/article/0,,2010 7971,00.html.

Jameson, W. C. *Buried Treasures of Texas.* Little Rock, AR: August House, 1991.

Littlejohn, E. G. "Lost Gold of the Llano Country." In *Legends of Texas,* edited by J. Frank Dobie, 20–23. Hatboro: PA: Folklore Associates, [1924] 1964.

Parks, H. B. "Buried in Bexar County." In *Southwestern Lore*, edited by J. Frank Dobie, 133–141. Dallas: Southern Methodist University Press, [1931] 1965.

San Saba News. "The Lost San Saba Mines." www.texfiles.com/texashistory/san_saba_mines.htm.

Syers, William Edward. *Off the Beaten Trail*. Waco, TX: Texian, 1971.

Townsley, Bill. "The Bowie Mine: A Literature Review." www .texfiles.com/texashistory/bowiemine.htm.

Unsolved Mysteries. "Alamo Treasure." www.unsolved.com/ treasure.html.

Weddle, Robert S. *The San Saba Mission: Spanish Pivot in Texas*. Austin: University of Texas Press, 1964.

Wilbarger, J. W. *Indian Depredations in Texas*. Austin, TX: Hutchings, 1889.

RETURN OF THE GHOST BUFFALO

Cox, Mike. "White Buffalo." www.texasescapes.com/ MikeCoxTexasTales/White-Buffalo.htm.

Fowler, Zinita. *Ghost Stories of Old Texas*. Austin, TX: Eakin, 1983.

Gard, Wayne. "How They Killed the Buffalo." *American Heritage*. www.americanheritage.com/articles/magazine/ah/1956/5/ 1956_5_34.shtml.

Houston Chronicle. "American Legend Is Made Flesh." September 24, 1994.

Powersource Gallery. "The Legend of the White Buffalo." www .powersource.com/gallery/whiteb.html.

Syers, William Edward. *Off the Beaten Trail*. Waco, TX: Texian, 1971.

"White Buffalo Days: Spirit of the West." www.snydertexas.net/whitebuffalo.aspx.

Williams, Docia Schultz. *Phantoms of the Plains: Tales of West Texas Ghosts.* Plano, TX: Wordware, 1996.

THE PACING WHITE STALLION

The Archives of the Michigan Museum of Ghost Wind Horse History. "Ghost Wind Stallions." http://indianspirithorses.com/ghostwindstallions.htm.

Cody, Betsy A. "Wild Horse and Burro Management." *CRS Report for Congress.* March 19, 1997. National Council for Science and the Environment. http://ncseonline.org/NLE/CRSreports/biodiversity/biodv-33.cfm.

Dan Patch Central. "Did You Know . . . ?" http://deckernet.com/minn/DanPatch.

Dobie, J. Frank. "The Deathless Pacing White Stallion." *The Best of Texas Folklore: 1916–1954,* edited by Mody C. Boatright, Wilson M. Hudson, and Allen Maxwell, 105–112. Denton: University of North Texas Press, [1954] 1998.

———. *The Mustangs.* Edison, NJ: Castle, 1952.

Melville, Herman. *Moby Dick.* New York: Easton, [1851] 1977.

Reid, Mayne. *The War Trail, or the Hunt for the Wild Horse.* London: J. & C. Brown, 1857. http://books.google.com.

U.S. Department of the Interior Bureau of Land Management. "Wild Horse and Burro Quick Facts." www.blm.gov/wo/st/en/prog/wild_horse_and_burro/Fact_Sheet.html.

Webb, W. P. "The White Steed of the Prairies." In *Legends of Texas,* edited by J. Frank Dobie, 221–226. Hatboro, PA: Folklore Associates, [1924] 1964.

BIGFOOT IN TEXAS

Burgan, Michael. *Bigfoot.* Mankato, MN: Capstone, 2005.

Cox, Greg. *Bigfoot.* New York: Rosen, 2002.

The Cryptozoologist. www.lorencoleman.com/cryptozoology_faq.html.

Dobie, J. Frank. *Tales of Old-Time Texas.* Austin: University of Texas Press, [1928] 1992.

Fowler, Zinita. *Ghost Stories of Old Texas.* Austin, TX: Eakin, 1983.

Lovett, Richard A. "Bigfoot in Texas? Believers, Skeptics Sound Off at Institute." *National Geographic News,* May 12, 2006. http://news.nationalgeographic.com/news/2006/05/bigfoot-texas.html.

Texas Bigfoot Research Conservancy. www.texasbigfoot exasbigfootgff

CHASING CHUPACABRAS

Catalano, Julie. "Chupacabra Capture in Blanco Puts Texas on the 'Mythical' Map Again." *Austin Small Town Travel Examiner,*

September 2, 2009. www.examiner.com/x-2427-Austin-Small
-Town-Travel-Examiner~y2009m11d24-Chupacabra-capture
-in-Blanco-puts-Texas-on-mythical-map-again.

"Chupacabra." www.sheppardsoftware.com/Mexicoweb/factfile/
Unique-facts-Mexico14.htm.

"Chupacabra: The Facts." www.lonympics.co.uk/chub.htm.

Cox, Mike. "Chupacabra." www.texasescapes.com/MikeCoxTexas
Tales/Chupacabra.htm.

"Cuero's Own Chupacabra . . . Fact or Fiction?" www.cuero
chupacabra.com.

KSAT-TV. "Chupacabra Craze Inspires Woman to Start Business,"
July 9, 2008. www.ksat.com/news/16831656/detail.html.

———. "DeWitt Sheriffs Think They've Seen the Chupacabra,"
August 11, 2008. www.ksat.com/news/17164217/detail.html.

———. "NW Side Man Claims to Have Seen Chupacabra,"
March 11, 2009. www.ksat.com/news/18911486/detail.html.

Mongabay. "Photos of Alleged Blood-Sucking Chupacabra Found
in Texas." http://news.mongabay.com/2007/0901-chupacabra
.html.

National Geographic. "Sucking Out the Truth." http://channel
.nationalgeographic.com/series/is-it-real/2509/facts.

Neer, Katherine. "How Chupacabras Work." http://science.how
stuffworks.com/chupacabra.htm.

Roldan, Steve. "Blanco Man Thinks He Has Chupacabra." KSAT San Antonio, August 31, 2009. www.ksat.com/news/206536 15/detail.html.

White, Elizabeth. "Monster or Dog? 'Goatsucker' Tale Debated." Associated Press, August 31, 2007. www.msnbc.msn.com/id/ 20539085.

LEGENDS OF ENCHANTED ROCK

Fowler, Zinita. *Ghost Stories of Old Texas*. Austin, TX: Eakin, 1995.

Kennedy, Ira. *The Enchanted Rock*. www.texfiles.com/enchanted rocktexas/enchantedrockhistory.

Kohout, Martin Donell. "Enchanted Rock Legends." *Handbook of Texas Online*. www.tshaonline.org/handbook/online/articles/ EE/lxe1_print.html.

Leatherwood, Art. "Enchanted Rock." *Handbook of Texas Online*. www.tshaonline.org/handbook/online/articles/EE/rje13_print .html.

1 Adventure. "Legend of Two Lovers at Enchanted Rock." www.1adventure.com/archives/000177.html.

Reid, Samuel C., Jr. *The Scouting Expeditions of McCulloch's Texas Rangers*. Philadelphia: G. B. Zieber, 1847.

Roy, Adam. "Climbing with the Spirits." www.travelsinparadise .com/travelarticle/enchanted-rock-texas.html.

Syers, William Edward. *Off the Beaten Trail*. Waco, TX: Texian, 1976.

Texas Parks and Wildlife Department. "Enchanted Rock State Natural Area." http://tpwd.state.tx.us/spdest/findadest/parks/enchanted_rock.

Wilbarger, J. W. *Indian Depredations in Texas*. Austin, TX: Hutchings, 1889.

Zelade, Richard. *Hill Country*. Lanham, MD: Lone Star, 1999.

THE LURE OF THE MARFA LIGHTS

Chariton, Wallace O., Charlie Eckhardt, and Kevin R. Young. *Unsolved Texas Mysteries*. Plano, TX: Wordware, 1991.

Eckhardt, C. F. "The Marfa Lights." www.texasescapes.com/CFEckhardt/Marfa-Lights.htm.

Fowler, Zinita. *Ghost Stories of Old Texas II*. Austin, TX: Eakin, 1992.

Fulcher, Walter. *The Way I Heard It: Tales of the Big Bend*. Edited by Elton Miles. Austin: University of Texas Press, 1959.

Levy, Tobin. "The Lure of Marfa." *Austin American-Statesman*, June 25, 2009, sec. D.

Miles, Elton. *Tales of the Big Bend*. College Station: Texas A&M University Press, 1976.

Smith, Julia Cauble. "Marfa Lights." *Handbook of Texas Online*. www.tshaonline.org/handbook/online/articles/MM/lxml.html.

Southwest Ghost Hunters. Investigation Report, May 18, 1991. www.sgha.net/tx/marfa/marfa.html.

Syers, Ed. *Ghost Stories of Texas*. Waco, TX: Texian, 1981.

Williams, Docia Schultz. *Phantoms of the Plains: Tales of West Texas Ghosts*. Plano, TX: Wordware, 1996.

Williams, O. W. *Alsate, the Last of the Chisos Apaches*. Privately printed pamphlet, 1–7. Reprinted in Virginia Madison, *The Big Bend Country of Texas* (Albuquerque: University of New Mexico Press, 1955), 35–37.

The Haunting of Jefferson

Ghost Village. "Murderous Mirror Message." www.ghostvillage .com/encounters/2004/08172004.shtml.

The Grove. "The Grove—Jefferson, Texas." www.thegrove-jefferson .com.

Jefferson Hotel. "Ghost Stories from the Historic Jefferson Hotel." http://historicjeffersonhotel.com/ghost.htm.

Long, Christopher. "Jefferson, Texas." *Handbook of Texas Online.* www.tshaonline.org/handbook/online/articles/JJ/hgj2.html.

Metz, Leon C. *Roadside History of Texas*. Missoula, MT: Mountain Press, 1994.

Pilcher, Walter F. "Diamond Bessie Murder Trial." *Handbook of Texas Online.* www.tshaonline.org/handbook/online/articles/ DD/jbd1.html.

Reitano, Victoria. "The Grove." *Haunted Historic Houses.* This Old House online. www.thisoldhouse.com/toh/photos/ 0,,20234518_20529661,00.html.

Syers, William Edward. *Off the Beaten Trail.* Waco, TX: Texian, 1971.

Tolbert, Frank X. *Tolbert's Texas.* Garden City, NY: Doubleday, 1983.

Williams, Docia Schultz. *Best Tales of Texas Ghosts.* Lanham, MD: Republic of Texas, 1998.

SPIRITS IN SAN ANTONIO

Aron, Paul. *Unsolved Mysteries of American History.* Thorndike, ME: G. K. Hall, 1997.

Choron, James L. "Dawn at the Alamo." www.texasescapes.com/ Paranormal/Alamo-Ghosts.htm.

Christensen, Jo-Anne. *Ghost Stories of Texas.* Auburn, WA: Lone Pine, 2001.

Goodwin, David. "Ghosts of the Alamo: History & Hauntings of One of America's Greatest Landmarks." *Haunted History.* 2005. www.militaryghosts.com/alamo.html.

Menger Hotel. http://mengerhotel.com

Straach, Kathy. "San Antonio Ghost Tours Lead to the Menger Hotel." *The Dallas Morning News*, October 23, 2008. www .dallasnews.com/sharedcontent/dws/spe/holidays/halloween/ stories/DN-menger.

Tingle, Tim, and Doc Moore. *Texas Ghost Stories: Fifty Favorites for the Telling.* Lubbock: Texas Tech University Press, 2004.

Weiser, Kathy. *Legends of America.* October 2005. www.legendsof america.com/TX-AlamoGhosts.html.

Williams, Docia Schultz. *The History and Mystery of the Menger Hotel.* Plano, TX: Republic of Texas, 2000.

Williams, Docia Schultz, and Reneta Byrne. *Spirits of San Antonio and South Texas.* Plano, TX: Wordware, 1993.

Wlodarski, Robert, and Anne Powell Wlodarski. *Spirits of the Alamo: A History of the Mission and Its Hauntings.* Plano, TX: Republic of Texas, 1999.

CHILDREN OF THE TRACKS

"Ghost Tracks." *Yelp.* www.yelp.com/biz/ghost-tracks-san-antonio.

"Ghost Tracks of San Antonio." *Weird U.S.* www.weirdus.com/ states/texas/road_less_traveled/children_of_the_tracks/index .php.

"Helping Hands." *Snopes.* www.snopes.com/horrors/ghosts/hand print.asp.

"Memorial to Mark 1938 Crash that Killed 23 Students." *The Salt Lake Tribune,* November 24, 2013. archive.sltrib.com/ story.php?ref=/sltrib/news/57173748/bus-jordan-driver -train.html.csp.

Mendoza, Madalyn. "Change Coming to San Antonio's Legendary 'Ghost Tracks.'" *mySA*. www.mysanantonio.com/news/local/article/San-Antonio-spook-hunters-will-be-stopped-in-6476017.php.

Rybczyk, Mark Louis. "Everything You've Ever Wanted to Know about San Antonio's Ghost Crossing." *San Antonio Uncovered*. www.sanantoniouncovered.com/2013/05/everything-you've-ever-wanted-to-know.html.

"San Antonio Ghost Children—DEBUNKED." *Spookannie*. spookannie.blogspot.com/2008/03/san-antonio-ghost-children.html.

"San Antonio, Texas: Ghostly Gravity Hill." www.roadsideamerica.com/tip/1298.

"Texas Legends: Ghost Children upon San Antonio's Railroad Tracks." *Legends of America*. www.legendsofamerica.com/tx-ghostlychildren.html.

Tingle, Tim, and Doc Moore. "Children of the Tracks." *Texas Ghost Stories: Fifty Favorites for the Telling*, 224–227. Lubbock: Texas Tech University Press, 2004.

Wagner, Stephen. "Haunted Railroad Crossing." paranormal.about.com/od/hauntedplaces/a/The-Haunted-Railroad-Crossing.htm.

Williams, Docia Schultz, and Reneta Byrne. "The Eerie Railroad Crossing." *Spirits of San Antonio and South Texas*, 30–32. Plano, TX: Wordware, 1993.

The Legendary Sally Skull

Block, W. T. "Sally Scull: Texas Pioneer 'Bad Girl.'" Texas Escapes. www.texasescapes.com/WTBlock/Sally-Scull-Texas-Pioneer -Bad-Girl.htm.

Coppedge, Clay. "Sally Skull." Texas Escapes. www.texasescapes .com/ClayCoppedge/Sally-Skull.htm.

Ford, John S. *Memoirs*. Austin: The University of Texas Archives IV.

Froebel, Joseph. *Seven Years Travel in Central America, Northern Mexico, and the Far West of the United States*. London: Richard Bentley, 1859.

Givens, Murphy. "Did Husband No. 5 Kill Sally Skull?" *Corpus Christi Caller Times*, June 29, 2011.

Kilgore, Dan. "Two Sixshooters and a Sunbonnet: The Story of Sally Skull." *Legendary Ladies of Texas*, edited by Francis Edward Abernethy, 59–71. Denton: University of North Texas Press, 1994.

Smithwick, Noah. *The Evolution of a State* or *Recollections of Old Texas Days*. Austin, TX: Gammel, 1900.

Van Ostrand, Maggie. "Texas Legends: Sally Skull—The Scariest Siren in Texas." Legends of America. www.legendsofamerica. com/tx-sallyskull/html.

The Hanging of Chipita Rodriguez

Fowler, Zinita. *Ghost Stories of Old Texas*. Austin, TX: Eakin, 1983.

Guthrie, Keith. *History of San Patricio County*. Austin, TX: Nortex, 1986.

Hebert, Rachel Bluntzer. *San Patricio de Hibernia: The Forgotten Colony*. Austin, TX: Eakin, 1981.

Ray, Steve. "Chipita's Execution Haunts Local Memory." *Corpus Christi Caller-Times*, February 2, 1998. www.caller2.com/newsarch/news10471.html.

Syers, Ed. *Ghost Stories of Texas*. Waco, TX: Texian, 1981.

Tingle, Tim, and Doc Moore. *Texas Ghost Stories: Fifty Favorites for the Telling*. Lubbock: Texas Tech University Press, 2004.

Underwood, Marylyn. "The Ghost of Chipita: The Crying Woman of San Patricio." *Legendary Ladies of Texas,* edited by Mody C. Boatright, Wilson M. Hudson, and Allen Maxwell, 51–56. Denton: University of North Texas Press, 1994.

———. "Josefa Rodriguez." *Handbook of Texas Online*. www.tshaonline.org/handbook/online/articles/RR/fro50.html.

THE LOVE STORY OF FRENCHY MCCORMICK

Cal Farley's Boys Ranch. "History of Old Tascosa." www.calfarley.org/visitors/Pages/TourismHistory.aspx.

Firman, Casandra. *One Christmas in Old Tascosa*. Lubbock: Texas Tech University Press, 2006.

Haley, J. Evetts. *The XIT Ranch of Texas: And the Early Days of the Llano Estacado*. Norman: University of Oklahoma Press, [1929] 1967.

Jent, Steven A. *A Browser's Book of Texas Quotations*. Plano, TX: Republic of Texas, 2001.

McArthur, Judith N. "Frenchy McCormick." *Handbook of Texas Online*. www.tshaonline.org/handbook/online/articles/MM/fmc21.html.

McCarty, John L. *Maverick Town: The Story of Old Tascosa*. Norman: University of Oklahoma Press, [1946] 1988.

Moore, Linda Sanderson. "Early Settlements in the Panhandle." *Accent West*, September 2009, 23–31.

Nolan, Frederick. *Tascosa: Its Life and Gaudy Times*. Lubbock: Texas Tech University Press, 2007.

Old Mobeetie Texas Association. "Frenchy McCormick." www.mobeetie.com/pages/frenchy.htm.

Robertson, Pauline Durrett, and R. L. Robertson. *Mystery Woman of Old Tascosa*. Amarillo, TX: Paramount, 1995.

———. *Panhandle Pilgrimage*. Canyon, TX: Staked Plains, 1976.

Syers, William Edward. *Off the Beaten Trail*. Waco, TX: Texian, 1971.

INDEX

ABOUT THE AUTHOR

Storyteller and author Donna Ingham is a collector of folklore, especially that of her home state. As a former college English professor, she's also a tireless researcher. She currently divides her time between touring as a performing storyteller and retreating to her study to write books like this one, her fourth for Globe Pequot/Lone Star Books. Ingham lives in Spicewood, Texas, with her husband, Jerry.